SAAB CELEBRATION

SWEDISH STYLE REMEMBERED

URSAAB

SAAB CELEBRATION

SWEDISH STYLE REMEMBERED

PHOTOGRAPHED & WRITTEN BY LANCE COLE

PEN & SWORD
TRANSPORT

AN IMPRINT OF PEN & SWORD BOOKS LTD.
YORKSHIRE - PHILADELPHIA

First published in Great Britain in 2021 by
Pen and Sword Transport
An imprint of
Pen & Sword Books Ltd
Yorkshire - Philadelphia

ISBN 978 1 52677 523 8

Typeset by SJmagic DESIGN SERVICES, India.

Printed and bound in India by Replika Press Pvt. Ltd.

Pen & Sword Books Ltd incorporates the Imprints of Pen & Sword Books Archaeology, Atlas, Aviation,
Battleground, Discovery, Family History, History, Maritime, Military, Naval, Politics, Railways, Select,
Transport, True Crime, Fiction, Frontline Books, Leo Cooper, Praetorian Press, Seaforth Publishing,
Wharncliffe and White Owl.

For a complete list of Pen & Sword titles please contact

PEN & SWORD BOOKS LIMITED
47 Church Street, Barnsley, South Yorkshire, S70 2AS, England
E-mail: enquiries@pen-and-sword.co.uk
Website: www.pen-and-sword.co.uk

Or

PEN AND SWORD BOOKS
1950 Lawrence Rd, Havertown, PA 19083, USA
E-mail: Uspen-and-sword@casematepublishers.com
Website: www.penandswordbooks.com

Contents

Acknowledgements

With thanks to all who have helped me and my Saab obsession over the years. For your support and tutelage, I offer thanks, not least to the following: Erik and Pat Carlsson, Chris Hull, Chris Partington, Alex Rankin, Rob Morley, Graham Macdonald, Martin Lyons, Chris Redmond, David Dallimore, Arthur Civill, David Lowe, Alan Sutcliffe, Mike Philpott, Tony Greystok, Jean Francois Bouvard, Alain Rosset, Tom Donney, Bruce Turk, Hilton Holloway, Mark McCourt, Richard Gunn, James Walshe, Steven Wade, Drew Beddelph, Peter Backström, Krysztof Rozenblat. The Västergötlands Museum, Sweden. The Saab Museum.

Dedication

With admiration and respect to the Saab heroes: Gunnar Ljungström, Sixteen Sason, Rolf Mellde, Björn Enval, Erik Carlsson, Stig Blomqvist, Gunnar Palm, Svante Holm, Tryggve Holm, Ragner Wahgren, Marcus Wallenberg, Sten Wenlo, Gunnar Dellner, Erik Rydberg, Enoch Thulin, Gosta Svenson, Sven Otterbeck, Hugo Moller, Gunnar Sjögren, Per Gillbrand, Robert Sinclair, Ralph Millet. Curt Mileikowsky, Jan-Ake Jonsson. There are other too numerous to mention (omissions are due to space not selection), but I salute you all, the philosophers and movers of the Svenska Aeroplan Aktie Bolaget.

Note: the photographer and author Lance F. Cole has no connection, nor affiliation of any kind to the website, claims, or actions, of 'Lance Cole Photography'.

Introduction

The classic Saab 96V4 RAC Rally tribute car bearing Stig Blomqvist's name and Swedish registration sticker. A car tweaked and owned (until recently) by the famed Saab restorer Graham Macdonald of Macdonald Classic Cars – with all that means to its brilliance: Macdonald has been restoring Saabs since the 1980s and is regarded as *the* 'old Saab 'person to go to. He may know more about fettling, mending and tuning these old cars than anyone in the UK. Note the US-spec headlamps, red paint, Bosch driving lamps, cabin cage, and emergency switches on the bonnet and you have classic 1970s Saabism. This car has now found a new custodian and will be seen in historic competitive events – minus its decals.

Saabism: ethos of engineering, design and ownership

Cars are cars and nothing else is intended. So goes the narrative about the inanimate lumps of steel, iron, aluminium, plastic and padding that are our motor cars. A car is just a car, or so it is said by rational and learned men, and don't they always know best?

Well, try telling that to the owner of a Saab, or a Citroën, a Porsche, an Allard, and Alvis, a Triumph, a Lancia, a Pierce Arrow, and NSU, or a whole host of other magnificent automotive names that characterise our cars and our affection for their supposedly inanimate forms.

The Saab is apparently, just a car. Yet tell that to an owner of an old Saab (or even a newer varietal), for the Saab car from its 1947 prototype onwards and its offspring is a marvellous collection of parts, designs, motifs, and engineering and design thinking. In their totality, welded up and fitted up into a car, all these elemental strands come together to create a motor car of huge personality, of distinct design language identity.

We Saabists hate our cars being called 'weird', 'quirky' or other such terms by the mainstream thinkers who have always seemed to want to use such terms: our Saabs are, simply, clever.

Jump in a Saab and drive off and you know you are somewhere different. There is something deeply primordial about an early Saab, especially an oily-rag car – one that is corroded, paint faded, and utterly original in all its unrestored beauty complete with a smelly cabin.

The Saab was never a consumer device that happened to have wheels – the fate of so many of our cars, especially today. Built-in obsolescence? Not at Saab. The foibles of fashion? Never, ever, at Saab, thank you. Accountancy-led philosophy – not at Saab, well, not until they took over via Detroit's influence. For Saab's men were engineers and designers, not marketing clinic chameleons greasing the corporate hierarchy with new speak and gobbledegook.

These Swedes had soul – and so did their cars.

The Swedish are an interesting lot and so too was their Saab. Safety, engineering integrity, environmental concerns, perfect design, all were part of the social science of Sweden decades before they became today's fashionable brand halos for corporates all over the world to proclaim. Such ingredients were also the essentials of Saab thinking and product design.

Swedes can be introvert, extrovert, free-thinking and yet conservative all at the same time. They and their Saabs are, as I say, very interesting. Or they were – before the brainwashing of coalition thinking and the narrative that denies one old culture and character in the name of globalised diversity, yet which, while denying that one culture's rights, insists on the promotion of another's. Saab and its old Swedes did not occupy such ground, however liberal and diverse you might imagine the Swedes to be. And without a touch of Swedish arrogance, Saab would never have been born. Oh, yes, the Swedes can be arrogant, and Saab was all the better for their belief in themselves and their values and their culture – like any other tribe anywhere in the world.

How do we account for the differences between the Saab philosophy and the different Volvo philosophy? Both Swedish, but both of opposing personality constructs and belief systems. Nothing wrong with Volvo of course, but they were not Saabs. Trollhättan versus Gothenburg, now that was another story. Front wheel-drive versus rear wheel-drive? Curves versus straight lines? Who knows? It must be something in the Swedish runes.

Beyond engineering and design psychology, then there is the *driving* of the Saab. From 92 to 96V4, from Sonett, from 99 to 900, thence to 9000, the Saab also drove and behaved in a specific manner, that primordial thing again. Oh, that wonderful rasping of the two-stroke at high revs, the uneven burble of the V4, the induction-combustion sound of the turbocharged cars, what audible characters these cars were.

The Saab process, this ownership affair of the heart as well as the mind, was the framework to recognise and understand 'Saabness' and its manifestation of 'Saabism' – a condition (some say a disease) that is caught by those so infected – the 'Saabists'. I am one of them. For Saab is carved upon my heart and upon what remains of the entrails of my finances. I think Citroën may be tattooed upon my posterior, but Saab is in my heart.

To me, sitting behind the wheel of a 93, a 96, or beside that great curved windscreen slot of the 99 and the 900, bolstered by an orthopaedic seat and protected by that high bulkhead somehow created a distinct Saabness, a deep connection to industrial design.

There is a sense of occasion in the driving or travelling in a Saab. It is an alchemy of Saab themes and traits that created the spirit of Saab. Those of you who share the experience will know that this is not hype, but true Saabness.

The later Saabs the cars cross-fertilised by General Motors DNA might not be quite so Saab 'pure' as their ancestors, but they too looked and went with a certain Saab character: the GM-controlled Saabness, although diluted a touch, remained to a degree. So despite the fact that the older Saabs might be called 'real' Saabs by some tribal purists, we should not dismiss the later, more recent Saabs – for they are Saabs, but just in a different way. Their owners are just as dedicated to their Saabs as the old purists and a 92, 96, 99 or classic 900.

Saab designers knew what made a Saab and, even under GM, the design genius of Michael Mauer gave us hope for Saab design after 2000. He now shapes cars for Porsche, the fortunate man. Anthony Lo influenced later Saab design, as did Simon Padian and Einar Hareide. They looked forward as well as back at the brilliance of Saab's Sixten Sason, and Björn Envall – the design setters of Saab. If only Lo's AeroX concept of a Sonett reborn could have been made. If only Mauer's 9-X had been taken to reality. Even at the last gasp, Jason Castroita's design concept for Saab under Muller as the Phoenix-X, was pure Saabism in all its elemental, being almost Darwinian in its evolution of the Saab species; of having that Saab primordial quality again.

However, I and my Saab friends cannot embrace the limited-run, last-gasp of the GM genetically modified and badge-engineered Subaru-Saabs and Chevrolet-Saabs. We cannot and we must not and if you disagree, then you do not understand Saab. Forgive me such arrogance and indulgence, but this is *my* book! And I have some Swedish DNA in my genes and have also worked for Saab. So my view is not confirmation bias, but confirmation experience and culturalism.

A Saab is a Saab, not a Subaru with a different badge: you are not going to argue or whinge on the web about that are you? Oh please…

Amid the compound curves of the true Saab, amid the elliptical excellence, inside the extra-safe highly torsionally rigid Saab, within its peppy two-stroke or its turbocharged thrust, conducted from its aircraft cockpit command post, there lies an ingredient as that found in old Porsche, Lancia or Citroën. In fact, a lot of Citroën fans are Saab fans and I know Citroën owners who also own old Saabs. Somehow both marques share an aura, a feel of old metal and new thinking. Wind-cheating ellipses and sculpted steel – both are of Citroën and of Saab. Safety? Well, that was a *Saab* speciality.

This is character, design, ethos, ability, identity and a defined design language not designed for those who do not wish to speak it.

Claims of being inspired by aviation design and technology are easy to make but harder to prove and manifest, but Saab cars really did use aircraft engineering in their philosophy. In case you have forgotten, Saab began in the 1930s as an aircraft maker, born from an industrial and transport concern going back decades. Ever heard of a Saab 90 Scandia? It was superb airliner that few have heard of, and yet they were operated as far afield as South America.

Incidentally, we ought to term Saab as S.A.A.B. (or SAAB) as those are the initials of its formative etymology – just as Fiat should be titled F.I.A.T. not Fiat. But we do not, so in keeping with an inaccurate fashion, I use the nomenclature of Saab not SAAB, herein. Svenska Aeroplan Aktie Bolaget is one hell of a mouthful too.

The Saab owner's relationship with his or her car became an emotional thing, and Saab owners were academically cited as having a deeper relationship, a greater loyalty to their cars and their brand than some other owners have with their marques and the cars that stem from them.

I once wrote an article about the 'smell' of Saab. The article was targeted at older, pre-1994 Saabs as cars made under older processes at the Saab factory. The reaction and the reader numbers to that on-line article were phenomenal. Saabs, it seems, not only had a certain smell, they had an identity.

From an early age, I was fascinated by Saab. I was also captured by old Citroëns and old Porsches: I suffered the same of old Lancias, old Peugeots, NSU's and other mid-twentieth century motors that were designed and defined by men, not by computers and a mind-set of digital authoritarianism to a prescribed formula that is entirely reliant on the opinions of those who set its rules. Talk about arrogant and self-limiting, but they cannot see it.

I first saw a Saab 93 in Africa as a child, then saw Saab 96 V4s careering through tropical rally stages. The sight and the sound of these cars made a mark upon a child. Back in the northern European topography, I encountered the Saab 99 with its highly-curved windscreen and its elegant curves and that amazing slot-like view from a perch sat under the high-dashboard and those 2.5mm thick, triple section triangulated rolled-steel roll-over proof windscreen pillars which were the strongest windscreen pillars ever made for a mass production saloon car. Its designer' Sixten Sason's aircraft interior that he lifted from a Saab aeroplane into the 99, just added to the moment.

I, like many, became captivated by the elements of the Saab.

I learned to drive on vintage Ford tractors on a farm as a young boy, and my first driving lessons were on that farm conducting a Land Rover Series One, a 1949 VW Beetle, and a 1960s Saab 96V4. It was the Saab 96 that taught me much, not least 'rallying' it around the muddy fields and uphill and down dale: oh, what a car. I think I was fourteen or nearly fifteen when that Saab and its driving captured me. Yet I also remained captivated by my grandfather's Citroën DS and its act of mechanical progress.

About three years later, I bought my first car, an early, steel-bumpered 1968 Saab 99. I followed it up a few weeks later with a 1970s Citroën GS. As far as I was concerned, these were two of the greatest car designs of their era. To say that I was in love with them was to put it mildly. Luckily, I was saved from such unhealthy and Saab-Citroën obsessive pursuits by a girl. I looked at her, not at my Saab and my Citroën, but have to admit, I had a wandering eye – one that reverted to fall-back upon my motor cars.

Shortly afterwards, I purchased a classic Saab 900. After that came another one; then upon my driveway came the turbocharged version, and then years later a lovely dark blue classic 900 GLi five-door, my best Saab ownership story. Then, post-millennium, came the GM-based new generation Saab 900/9-3 which looked fantastic with its Envall inspired exterior and interior designs, but sadly had the build quality of a shopping trolley. I risked a 9-3 Mk2 – the saloon 9-3 based upon more of a GM platform than any Saab before (a platform with much secret Saab engineering work hidden deep within it). Frustratingly, while it drove well, it was unreliable and felt thin. Still, a 9-3 TurboX was not to be sniffed at, was it?

Along the way, back in 1989, I had found myself the driver of a Saab 9000i (Injection) – *not* the multi-valve Turbo variant, but the sweet running, well-mannered, injected 9000 base model. It was smoke silver metallic with a dark maroon interior. I loved its abilities, its simplicity, its balance and its brilliance. This car really felt like a true Saab, despite its Fiat-shared 'Type Four/Tipo Quattro' project origins. I later spent some time with the 9000 Turbo and loved it, but, do you know what, that 9000i was fantastic in all its facets of mechanism and operation. 9000 was one of the best Saabs yet was sadly a touch obscured by a narrative. To me, 9000 was one of the most balanced and most endearing cars of its era, yet few beyond the enclave realised it.

Twenty years later, Saab lent me a new 9-3 TTID to drive around Tasmania in 2009 when I met up with Mr Wade of *Saabs United*, the social media blog in its nascent days as *Trollhättan Saab*. The TTID was a great car and a great drive, and it felt and drove like a Saab, but there was just something missing, that tangible Saabness. Local Tasmanian Drew Beddelph took me off to his garage and showed me his little-known collection of old Saabs. What stories do such secret Saabs hide?

Reverting to a classic 900T for my Australian foray felt 'right' from the moment I leapt in it and drove off. I was back in a Saab that somehow spoke to me. Pilots of aircraft and yachtsman and ship captains will know exactly what I mean.

Saab remains a huge enthusiasm in Australia. Every state has its own Saab Club as part of the Saab Car Club of Australia that keeps the spirit of Saab alive, It was in Australia that the special 900 'Enduro' was created, with its glass fibre wide-bodied modifications and performance enhancements. 900 Enduro was a rare special edition by Saab Australia (wider wheels and suspension, water-injection to the turbocharger, and a modified wastegate) and few people have seen one of this rare species of Saab. Only eleven 900 Enduros were built, but later body kit conversions from an Adelaide dealer swelled the numbers.

Classic 900 just sounds, feels and drives right. An older Porsche 911 or a 356 offers the same sensation, as does a Lancia Fulvia, A Rover P6, or an NSU Ro80. Cocooned within the old Saab 900, everything is as it should be. You establish a deep connection to the machine.

Somehow, the inanimate object had life. Driving the classic Saab was to me akin to the moment I piloted a Vickers VC10 and, also the occasion I flew a Boeing 747-400; utter engineering and design perfection achieved in the action of mechanism and command.

I suppose I better admit that I have also owned Volvos, notably Volvo estates, and while they were different beasts to the Saab, they were not without merit. Volvos built in Sweden the Swedish way by the same gene pool that built Saabs, also had build-quality and safety. But new Volvos no longer feel like past Volvos, and neither did newer Saabs feel like past Saabs. I gave up on Volvo and my V70s at model year 2005. I gave up on Saab at model year 2000 and a bit. These days, I hanker for an old 99 or a 96, but a 900 classic would more than suffice. I am afraid I do not yearn for 2008 1.9Tid-engined Saab of late GM DNA. But if you do, I do not judge you.

Of the 'new' 9-5, the very last Saab back in 2010-2012? It looked brilliant, it drove well, and I wanted a black one. But, once again, the fit and finish were not of old Saab. The base model seats were not the Saab-standard orthopaedic jobs we were used to either. I wanted a new, 'last' Saab, but then *all* of my friends who had bought one found themselves paying out large sums of money to have their cars repaired. Yet was not that last-ever Saab, the 9-5 V6 Turbo four wheel drive (with Johansson engineering inherent), a wonderful car, a truly super Saab? Of course it was. But things went awry, I am afraid. Get a good one and have happy days, but many are of intermittent quality. Don't blame Mr Muller! Others were at fault.

Amid the falling entrails of Saab, my telephone rang and it was the BBC's *Top Gear* programme. A Mr Richard Porter was on the line. He wanted to know (having read one of my books on Saab) if it was correct that you could drop a proper, classic Saab 900 on its roof from a height of eight feet and that the roof would not crush down? I confirmed that Saab had built-in rollover bars made of 2.5mm rolled solid steel triangular sections (as the strongest production car roof pillars made) into its Saab 900's windscreen pillars and that yes eight feet was the height Saab had tested the original 900 at (and its forebear the 99).

'Jeremy (Clarkson) wants to know if we can drop it from eleven feet' said Mr Porter.

'Why' I asked, thinking, how typical...

'Because eight feet seems pretty average and wouldn't most cars survive a drop from eight feet, I mean there is legislation about roof strength.' said Mr Porter.

I drew breath and replied: 'No. The later American crash-test guidelines demanded a three foot drop height to test a vehicle's roof crush strength and the earlier legislation only demanded a one foot drop.'

'You are joking, three feet! But the Saab 900 and its ancestor the 99 come from thirty years ago or more, they cannot be that much stronger in today's safety market!'

Such was the response.

'Well, the industry set the standards and, as you know, the likes of Saab, Volvo, Mercedes Benz, Rover, and a few others decided long ago to voluntarily exceed the tests requirements. It's why the current Volvo XC90 has a titanium roof with roll-over anti-crush design, whereas the big American and Japanese SUV equivalents did not. Try a roof drop with an old Ford Explorer and see what happens,' I said – knowing how the Explorer had been the subject of American media interest in its allegedly poor roll-over roof crush crash test.

'What if we get another, similar type of car and drop it from eight feet and then do the same to the Saab. Will that work?' asked Mr Porter.

'Yes, although another Swedish car or German make might be more resilient to the drop than an American or Japanese or Korean car. It's up to you.' I replied.

The telephone call ended and a few months later, this particular episode of *Top Gear* was broadcast, and it dropped a quality German car, a BMW 3-Series on its roof from eight feet.

The results were astounding – the BMW's roof crushed right down onto the dashboard and seat tops. Any chance of the occupants surviving the resultant head, lumbar and thoracic injuries would have been slight indeed. So, even a BMW was flattened when dropped from eight feet onto its roof. I had thought a BMW might do better… I knew that many other cars would simply be flattened as if put in a scrapper's crusher. But a BMW *had* suffered under roof crush load…

Next up, came the Saab 900 Classic five-door – an 'old' car design dating back to the late-1970s and in fact based on a Saab 99 designed in the mid-1960s. Clearly, Messrs, J. Clarkson, and J. May, were sceptical. So the Saab was dropped hard onto its roof from eight feet and, guess what? With some minimal deformation the roof stayed upright and intact, the vital windscreen pillars (A-pillars) and the middle (B-pillars) stayed rigid. The occupants' survival space and headspace were retained, even the doors opened. Clarkson, and particularly May, were suitably impressed: May really was amazed.

In fact, due to its front-end heavy design and lack of rear-end weight and minus fuel in its tank, the Saab loaded up its windscreen pillars even harder by dropping front-first onto the front of its roof – so the load was not spread evenly front to rear onto the roof. This was a tougher test. But the doors opened, the roof stayed up and survival space was maintained.

So Saab safety was proven for a worldwide audience. Curiously, this Saab-v-BMW roof drop-test film footage was cut from the broadcast edit of the perpetual repeat of this *Top Gear* 'Saab tribute' episode as now repeatedly aired on another channel. I still wonder why.

Car safety is, as demonstrated above, a strange thing: an ancient old Saab had a stronger roof and windscreen pillars than even a newer type of BMW. What legislation, indeed, what practices allowed this to happen? Imagine if the other car had not been a BMW but some flimsy old lightweight car of thin skinning and thin structure from somewhere near Detroit or Tokyo or Seoul?

But that was then, and *Top Gear* said goodbye to Saab, as we Saabists have now also done.

The end of Saab was a sad affair and the fashion for blaming one man was unfair. There were many more tangents to the recipe that ended the Saab car story than Mr Muller's often credible (but sometimes challengeable) efforts: General Motors somehow just did not seem to understand Saab thinking, and finally sold it with caveats and bridles attached, all of which was a surprise given the company's excellent guidance of Opel and its cars for decades. Does anyone remember the 1980s Opel Monza and the Opel Senator? They were fine motor cars which were obscured by badge snobbery and fixed marketing mind sets.

Opel's Monza was a gem, a true GT tourer and so elegant and also highly aerodynamic; Monza was a clever a car and one of Opel's best ever. Yet Saab and Opel's men failed to find their own gem, and GM's Detroit bean-counters and engineers of fixed thinking, failed to set Saab free to be what they had bought the brand and its badge for in the first place. The paradox was frustrating.

GM did not even reskin its Opel Astra (a fine handling car) into a new smaller, mass market Saab that was so needed in that sector. It could have been so easy to do at minimal cost – just as VW did to the Skoda out of the VW parts bins. Yet just such an idea was sketched up in the styling studio: with thought and typical cleverness from the Saab design team, Astra could have become something more convincing than a badge engineered platform-derived marketing con. It could have provided a floorpan and drivetrain for a brilliant new small Saab. But no, GM spent hundreds of millions on badge engineering old Opels, existing Subarus, and even an old truck of a Chevy Blazer, into 'fake' Saabs. Turning an Astra into 'new' Saab 96 would have been a much better idea. But people know what they know and are often trapped by perceived wisdom – itself a self-limiting contradiction in terms.

Saab's appeal to 'Move your mind' was great, but not when applied to a re-badged Subaru or a Chevrolet, surely? Not even the undoubted talent of Bob Lutz could save Saab from a re-badged Saab-aru nor a Chevrolet-tagged Saab –even if it did have added 'Saabness' from Saab's brilliant engineers.

Oh, how all those millions could have been better spent.

In the interests of balance, I have to say that, to me, even Trollhättan's 'old guard' Saab men had their own share of blame for what happened to Saab in the 1980s and 1990s *prior* to GM, or Muller ownership of the beloved brand. For Saab's own true, Swedish guiders, failed to re-enact the ethos of their founding success – a small sporty, characterful car designed to be of lower cost and distinct Swedish type – but not a Volvo. If Saab had reinvented their 92-96 range for the modern era, it would have had a domestic, European and global bestseller on its hands because it would have been a small-to-medium-sized sporty little hatchback with the combined appeal of a VW Golf crossed with an Alfa Romeo Alfa Sud, with a touch of Fiat and Citroën and Renault thrown in, when all these cars makers made such successful and profitable cars.

Imagine a mass-market small, family Saab hatchback circa 1990 onwards (and in subsequent iterations) one that included all the ingredients of these cars but with added Saabness! It would have sold two or three million examples and returned Saab to profitability. But it was not to be. Instead, Saab went upmarket – understandably so for the American market (Robert Sinclair of Saab America was not wrong), but regretfully in the rush to turbocharging and then bigger cars with bigger engines, Saab did not cater for its original, core buyer base with a smaller, sporty, unique Saab that a reinvented 96 could have been.

Saab knew this and catered for the factor by welding the front the old 99 to the back of the slightly less old 900 and calling it a 'new' car – the 90. It was a true Saab but, in all honesty, was it not a con-trick destined to fail, perhaps in the manner of a badge-engineered excess of desperate measure? Still, at least it was not an Allegro Vanden Plas.

So ended a wonderful story of Saab – as the Swedish-owned car maker that had also made aircraft. Scania's (including Scania-Vabis) history helped in the Saab-Scania years, but in the end, after a brief sniff from Fiat, Saab was snapped up by GM and the men in Detroit who knew what they knew and did not want to know anything else, as seen from their bubble of self-professed exceptionalism.

So it was that Saab's problems began long before GM stepped into the ring of blame and a possible merger with Volvo had receded upon the tides of solely Swedish issues. But, pre-GM, we did get the brilliant Saab 9000 which really was a super Saab despite some shared Fiat underpinnings. My belief is that the 9000 *was* a 'real' Saab and a very good one, a car touched by Saab's top team of engineers and designers as a last fanfare to 'real' Saab.

9000 was Envall-designed and Saab engineered and much stronger than its Fiat-based brethren.

Some say the last 'real' Saab was the classic 900. Personally, although I adore that car, my own view is that the last 'pure' Saab was the excellent 9000. But many Saabists will shout and defend the later GM Saab varietals as real Saabs. Well, maybe but maybe not. Let's agree to disagree and just enjoy Saab. Let us celebrate the sadly departed Saab, its ethos and its cars.

Here, we celebrate all that was Saab, older and later.

I would like to take the opportunity to thank some Saab heroes and some younger Saab enthusiasts – my friends and colleagues across club life and motoring journalism. For all over the world there are Saab fans. They, I, and you, love Saab and its Saabs.

Did you know that Queen Beatrix of Holland once drove Saabs, as did the Swedish Royal family, led by Prince Bertil, and the Danish royals followed the example. Mr Rutter the Dutch prime Minister is a Saab owner. So too was the famous British comedian Eric Morecombe. Ex-Spitfire pilot and BBC broadcaster Raymond Baxter owned a Saab too. Top BBC man Jonathan Stedall drove a Saab and John Betjeman (whom Stedall knew and made superb programmes about) loved riding in it apparently: imagine old Betjeman sitting in the Saab's front passenger seat – come friendly Saab, to Cornwall we must go.… .

Many other 'names' have owned Saab's as their private cars – Peter Ustinov, Stephen Fry, Richard Branson, Björn Borg, members of Abba, and others were Saabists. Even arch-cynic Jeremy Clarkson professed admiration for Saab.

In case you do not know, a certain Kurt Vonnegut once sold Saabs prior to his other career.

Saabs can be found in Africa, the outback of Australia and even the islands of the Pacific. America was and remains a huge Saab sanctuary and we must mention the Saab Club of North America, and also tribute Saab racer and restorer Tom Donney, his Saab collecting and his new Saab museum at Sturgis South Dakota. The man is a Saab saint and typical of the Saab passion and its people – who are all different, but who all love their Saabs. Donney is the man who took a 96 and also a Sonett to crazy record-setting speeds on the salt flats at Bonneville: Tom Donney is instrumental in the remembering of Saab. We owe him much.

Bruce Turk is another big time American Saab supporter and driver. Bruce is the founder of a movement and leads the Vintage Saab Club of North America. His addiction to old Saabs is a commitment that many admire. His barn full of Saabs – 93B, 96 two-stroke, other 95-96 types and, his stunning Sonett collection mark out one man's utter love of old Saabs. He drives his 96 'stroker' rally car with the sheer elan and pace of a true Saab rally professional.

The Vintage Saab Racing Group make sure their Saabs are driven as intended. The Saab Sonett was a big hit with enthusiasts in 1970s America and more recently Chris Moberg has collected numerous Sonetts on his Sonett ranch and runs a dedicated Saab Sonett website. Chris Mills is well known for his Spirit of Saab website and also the New England Saab Association. So Saab remains close to the hearts of its Saabsists Stateside.

Remember, at one moment of the 1980s, Saab sold more Saabs in America than it did in Sweden. Saab collectors still abound across the vast American landscape, but notably on the eastern seaboard. People like Jon Liland who owns a Porsche, a Mercedes Benz and a BMW, have little old Saabs secreted away for their moments of motoring joy, a place of happiness that is Saab-shaped. Liland has a 96 two-stroke for pure driving enjoyment. A Monte Carlo model no less. He had an early Sonett too.

American motoring journalist Mark McCourt, writing over the years for Hemmings the Vermont-based publisher, is a true Saabist who has championed Saab in a modern idiom to the marque's American fans. He too is a dedicated owner and supporter and believes in what he calls Saab's 'smart engineering'. The US East Coast is where Saab America established itself back in the mid-1950s.

American Saab also owes a lot to Robert 'Bob' Sinclair who was instrumental in the expansion of Saab and its legend in America. His Saab career began under Ralph Millet who was the man who originated the supply of Saabs for sale to the United States of America in the 1950s. Sadly, Sinclair died long before he should have done, and no recollection of Saab can ignore Bob Sinclair because he became 'Mr Saab' in America. He had vision and thought of the 900 cabriolet; he also built himself a Saab-powered motorcycle with a Saab two-stroke engine mounted in a BSA Rocket III frame.

Sometimes, Millet, and then Sinclair and his ilk found Saab's Swedish view of itself and the world somewhat frustrating. But Saab was Saab and that was that.

British motoring writer Hilton Holloway has done likewise at *Autocar* and always supported the Saab philosophy. We owe both men a salute for their Saabness. Like me, Holloway also has a penchant for Citroëns.

Richard Gunn, the motoring writer, promotes Saabism, and he likes old Citroëns and old Leyland products too. James Walshe at *Practical Classics* likes a Saab. Ian Fraser at *Car* magazine about three decades or more ago was a massive Saab fan, as was *Car*'s one time editor Mel Nichols. *The Automobile* liked Saabs and I wrote a big tribute to Saab for that magazine's 30th Anniversary issue, but sadly the publication subsequently behaved very badly indeed, so I cannot wish them a happy 40th. You never can tell, can you…

The late Erik Carlsson was of course the global 'Mr Saab' and I owe him and his late wife Pat Moss Carlsson a debt of gratitude to being so kind to me in my younger days. Thanks also to the unknown rally driver 'Mrs Johns' whom Pat knew, and so did I as a child. There are many others who have been so kind and helped nurture and support my Saab obsession.

Erik and Pat were wonderfully kind to lots of Saab fans, including me and it was my privilege to write Erik's obituary feature for the *Daily Telegraph*, and to attend his memorial service and the ensuing gathering which was so special and Erik. Having a personal cup of tea and a chat sat with Stirling Moss and Gunnar Palm was a high never to be forgotten. These men were true heroes of perhaps the best age of motoring and also the best era of England under the greatness of Queen Elizabeth in the 1960s.

Erik and Pat embodied the spirit of Saab; their daughter is made of the same stuff.

Björn Envall was my hero too and encouraged my design work and that of others. Thanks, Björn, you are a great man, an essential Saabist to whom we owe so much. Oh, to have met Sixten Sason: what a designer.

The Saab Museum at Trollhättan was an early exponent of the modern museum philosophy; we nearly lost the museum in the carve-up of Saab, but, thankfully, it survives, and Peter Backstrom and his colleagues keep the flame alive. Please support the Saab Museum.

I would like to tribute a few names of British Saabism here, people who love Saabs, notably older Saabs. They make up the core of the Saab movement here and are: Graham Macdonald, Chris Hull, Alex Rankin, Robin Morley, David Dallimore, Chris Redmond, Martin Lyons, Chris Partington, David Lowe, William and Bridget Glander, and others too numerous to mention. Thanks so much for all your kindness. Those of you in the various Saab clubs know who you are – even as far away as Australia, Uruguay, and Argentina, where Saabs are adored and still rallied. Some of you are named herein in the Acknowledgements, others are out there.

Above all, we are all Saab believers, Saabists of Saabism, a disease for which there may be no cure, no respite, except of course the painful reality that Saab, one of the greatest engineering and design institutions of man's motoring, has long departed. I hope my photographs evoke some kind of memory – in memoriam.

Thanks Saab. Saab that was more than a car, more than a company: Saab enthusiasm was and remains a band of brothers (and sisters) the world over, truly a great enthusiasm. Saab, you are gone now, and the pain shall only change, it will never depart. For Saabs were more than cars – they really were. Saabism is all we have left amid the sheer enjoyment of Saabs.

Lance Cole

A Saab 95 two-stroke long nose, chrome motifs, and grey paint. It says it all.

Above: Incoming! David Dallimore's 99 Turbo in black: classic Envall-style seen on the essential icon of 1970s-1980s-era Saab. Note the rising line to the rear of the bodywork framed by light.

Right: The original Saab emblem – with the Saab aircraft profile used to underpin the origins of the Svenksa Aeroplan Aktiebolaget.

Left: SAAB! Old grilles are often the best grilles.

Below: 96 two-stroke 'rasper' 24 NPO is an ex-Chris Partington car of special specification and is now run by David Lowe. This blue baby is primordial Saab personified. Get that down-the-road-graphic and sculpted stance.

Sonett spelt the Swedish design way. Sonett III interior in all its rarity. Crackled black plastic and tan leather: Sonett was a world away from the usual perception of Saab.

Custard dream: Sonett III in a typical 1970s hue shows off the unique styling from the days when Saab made a low-slung two-door, fastback coupé of a car. If only it had been reinvented…

Saab diversity. A 99 Turbo seen alongside the later 1996, 9000 Griffin specification and owned by Saab addict and fettler Chris Hamley. Both were Envall designs and both were 'proper' Saabs. Both went like stink and had that elusive ingredient of 'Saabness'.

Opposite: Saab then and now as two green 96s watch over a GM-era 9-3 convertible in that lovely Cerulean blue hue. Decades apart they maybe, but they framed the Saab brand in their respective contexts.

Above: Late model classic 900 Ruby specification hastens away in all its glory. This was timeless design at its best. Thanks Björn.

Left: Saab 9-3 TTID Mk2 seen at rest in Tasmania during the author's 2008-2009 Saab tour of Australia. A GM-era Saab it may have been, but it had enough of Saab in it to make it a good car. Tasmania by Saab – a joy never to be forgotten.

How could you not smile at this! The 95 pickup or ute. Simon Coleman's oily-rag special conversion has now been repainted in a all-over Saab blue and looks fantastic, yet this earlier non-paint job iteration, seen here at Prescott hill-climb, had a certain something did it not Simon? Saab Service, Saab Shop, Saab Style… SDV 188N is often confused with the similar PUY772L, but the word is that they are not the same car.

The faces of Saab: sheer character across the decades.

16 valve head on a slant-angled 'four' that had Triumph-Saab-Ricardo origins in the mid-1960s yet ended up pioneering the use of reliable turbocharging in a mass production car. How typically Saab.

1

92.001-96: Early Saabism

The first Saab car looked like a wing with wheels; a UFO of a car in new age of post-war technology and design. This was no accident nor was it a fashionable feint. It was science and Saab style in its first iteration. So began, from 1947, the original Saab or 'URSaab' as the Swedes would say.

Why was this car unlike any other car in the world? Have we forgotten that its shape was as revolutionary as was the Citroën DS's several years later in 1955?

Many post-war cars were reinventions of pre-war cars. Slowly, design and styling evolved but into fashion, rarely into aerodynamic design. In America,

the influence of the jet age and spaceship thinking manifested as wings, fins, intakes and bling, but rarely did it offer aerodynamic advantage. In Europe, a few car makers created their own design language, but hardly any car maker apart from Saab, Panhard, Citroën, Porsche, or Bristol, actively pursued aerodynamic design for road cars. But Saab was, in 1947, ahead of even Citroën, let alone Panhard or Porsche.

URSaab 92.001, the car that became the the 96, set a style and function that lasted from 1949 into the 1980s. Not only was the car aerodynamic, it was so strong it remained 'safe' into the new safety age of the car.

So radical was the Saab that even *Autocar* magazine remarked upon its radicalism, its different appearance and design formula. Surely, if this car had come from Detroit, or Paris, or Turin, much more fuss would have been made of it. But Trollhattan is a long way north and easily ignored.

In Britain, the British were producing re-warmed versions of 1930s cars up into the 1950s. Issigonis and his Mini were a revolution, but he was not British, not locked into class certainty, model hierarchy and badge snobbery.

Blue 96 Saab seen head-on: essential Saab design captured.

But we cannot say that the Saab car design was as it was because it was Swedish, because Swedish Volvo was producing Swedish cars and they were heavily influenced by American trends into the period 1946 to 1960-somehting. So how come Saab's Swedish car was so different, so utterly radical?

Everything else including Volvos (bar Citroëns and one or two rarities) was rear wheel drive, cart-sprung, slab-side, upright, boxy, or boxy with a fastback, or oblong with added fins as frippery. Yes, Monsieur Deutsch and Monsieur Bonnet were soon creating slippery, lozenge-shaped Panhards and their jointly initialled DB branded cars, but in 1950, not even Citroën had created its space-ship of car that was Bertoni's DS.

We have to ask ourselves, how come the Saab was as it was? And let's not forget that this was Saab's first car, its first ever attempt at a mass market family car!

The answer lay in art, Art Deco, Swedish craft design and industrial design, aircraft engineering, a German DKW car born of a Danish man named Rasmussen, and a series of circumstances that brought some clever men together. Add in some spice and something special happened.

Having emerged from a railway locomotive and stock building heritage, early trucks or prime movers, then the producing of military materials – notably aircraft built under licence from external suppliers, the company that became the Swedish Aviation (SA) Construction Company – the Svenksa Aeroplan (AB) morphed into an amalgamated brand, a national concern named SAAB – or Saab as we seem to now insist upon. Saab began via Scania, Vabis, Bofors, Nohab, Thulin, Nydqvist, Koppaberg, and the Svenska Jarnvagsverkstdaderna – the Swedish Railway Works as ASJA, all of them as the leading names of Swedish industrial companies and engineering experience, many focused on the city of Trollhättan and its hydro-electric works and expertise in such engineering and beyond. Nearby, the town of Linkoping also played a relevant role for these companies.

Enoch Thulin and his Aero Enoch Thulin Aeropanfabrik AETA Company had employed over 1,000 people building aircraft by the 1920s. Soon, he would merge with other like-minded men to create the Svenska Aeroplan (AB) in the 1920s. A merger of all the players in 1932 created the first iteration of a big Swedish conglomerate, but further industrial rationalisation would take place by state edict in 1936 under Premier Per-Albin Hanson. Thrown together were all they key players mentioned earlier, and so began the SAAB or Saab as an entity and a brand.

Behind all this lay the Wallenberg family of bankers and investors: they also owned a shipping line, transport stocks, and the Swedish rights to Rudolph Diesel's engine design.

So pivotal were the Wallenbergs and their Stockholms Enskilda Bank that they are deemed to be an essential part of Saab.

Swedes would in the 1920s-1930s licence built British, American and German aircraft, added 'improvements' and created a Swedish air transport arm of military and ultimately civil influence. Soon Saab would design and build its own aircraft that had hints of Bristol Dornier and Caprioni aircraft designs. This Saab Type 17 aircraft also incorporated American aviation ideas but was reputedly built to much tighter tolerances and weight constraints than American industry had then achieved.

The Swedes even imported an American car of the Continental brand and modified it for Swedish conditions. Soon, a DKW car of economy and ability would dominate Swedish pre-1939 motoring.

2 April 1937 was when Saab really began. Inside the new company were Swedish, German, and notably, British engineers.

After the interregnum of the Second World War, Saab had, by 1947, concocted its recipe for a special type of new car. Various bits, spare parts (from DKW, Auto Union and others), and handmade prototype toolings, came together to create a one-off that would become a world famous car. Less than twelve dedicated men were the core Saab car project team and a Mr Ljungström was the vital person.

Gunnar Ljungström

Of note was a young stress engineer and designer named Gunnar Ljungström who had trained in Sweden and in Great Britain at the A.J. Wickham Company and had returned to Sweden to join the nascent Saab via the Nohab company.

When the Second World War ended and Saab was desperate for something to build, produce, sell and earn, wing designer Ljungström would become the pivotal engineering figure for the new idea – the Saab car. In fact, he was the 'father' of the Saab car in engineering terms.

In 1945, Saab President Ragnar Wahgren led the decision to build a car – but a new car of a new Swedish design, not a hotch-potch of ancient, pre-war themes and thinking. Swedish car dealer and DKW seller Gunnar V. Philipson pumped in investment funds and the Saab car project was born. Saab aircraft leader Sven Otterbeck led the project and he pushed Ljungström to the front.

Gunnar Ljungström was an engineer with vision and a dedication to engineering and Swedish thinking. His father had been an engineer and inventor who had held patents for his hydro-power and agricultural engineering mechanisms inventions. He had also designed a new type of gearbox which his son Gunnar tried to further.

After graduating in 1932, Gunnar went to England to serve some time at A.C. Wickham Ltd – engineers. He then returned to Sweden with a mind full of ideas. He would work with famed Saab aircraft designer A.J. Andersson and worked on solving engine cooling and engine airflow problems (Jaguar's later designer Malcom Sayer would be doing the same at the Bristol Aircraft Company a few years later). Ljungström then concentrated on wing design, focusing not just on aerofoils but wing structure, weight, strength, and performance. It was this work that manifested in the body of hull of the Saab car prototype from 1947 after he had been asked to join the car project at its initial development stage.

As with an aircraft wing or fuselage, Ljungström designed the Saab car body to be very stiff in its key sections and to have reinforcements around openings and windows. This was why the Saab 92 had steel reinforcing rails in its windscreen pillars and very strong box sections around the door apertures. Thick sills and closed-off bulkheads meant that the cabin cell was many times stiffer than any car made at the time or for decades afterwards. Ljungström's key fellow men on his prototype development of the car's body were Olle Lindgren and Erik Ekkers. Josef Eklund would join Saab in 1953 and work with Ljungström to develop gearboxes and engines as the 92 evolved – soon to become the 93.

To prove that point, witness the 92's monocoque torsional rigidity rating: this was over 11,000 lbs/ft/degree. Even other monocoque-bodied cars at that time struggled to achieve 3,000 lbs/ft/degree of torsional rigidity. Over a decade later, Ford's 1960s (super-computer-designed) Cortina Mk1 managed 2,500 lbs/ft/degree – put plainly, it was less than a quarter as stiff in the body as the late-1940s designed Saab. Today, some modern cars exceed 6,000 lbs/ft/degree of torsional rigidity – just over half that which Saab achieved. The Saab used metal that was in places over 20 per cent thicker than the standard gauge. Thick side-sills and doors and reinforcing fillets all added to the car's supreme strength. Remember, this car remained 'safe' in legislative and crash terms into the 1980s.

The 92-96 was crush-proof and had anti-intrusion and roll-over strength that kept the cab safe and the roof upright when impacted. A roll-cage was added for legislative reasons for rally car Saabs, but so stiff was the car's cabin that you could roll one several times and drive away with the roof uncrushed – as Erik 'on-the-roof' Carlsson proved several times. When a Ford Cortina was dropped on its roof to prove how strong the Cortina rally car was, the results were embarrassing, in a flattening manner.

Intriguingly, the Saab 92 was not too stiff at the front of the car, so, with a softer, crushable nose, it offered some early degree of crash energy crumple zone – reducing the energy forced into the cabin and its occupants. Neither was 92 a heavy lump, it came in at under 900kg in road-use specification, vital given its tiny engine.

Saab 92 was shaped like a wing and the Swedes called it the 'Vingprofil' car. It was not just shaped like a wing, it was built like a wing. Saab 92 was a curved, ellipsoid, scaled piece of genius that was truly a new design statement in an austerity world. Under the skin it was clever too.

Ljungström worked on developing the 92-96 across the decades and influenced the Saab 99 – itself even stronger in the cabin and windscreen pillars than the 92-96 series. He worked on drivetrain components and suspension too. In fact, Ljungström touched many aspects of Saab car development, not least aerodynamics. Ljungström fitted the 92 with its flat-bottomed undertray and sculpted wheel shrouds and roof design. Gearboxes? Cylinder head design? Both were further areas of Ljungström's expertise for Saab. So too was the choice to go with a front-engine and a front wheel-drive configuration – before the so called 'revolutionary' Mini with its front wheel-drive of the late 1950s.

Yet Ljungström was no designer of bodywork and his own sketches to shape the first Saab car were good, but he knew they were not good enough which was very self-aware of him. Enter Sixten Andersson – who had in fact changed his last name to Sason – Sixten Sason.

Sixten Sason

Born in 1912 and through youthful training as a pilot in the Swedish Air Force in the early 1930s, Karl Erik Sixten Sason became fascinated by aircraft. He was injured in a flying accident and a wing strut penetrated his chest. Minus one lung and struck down by infection, he recovered by re-inventing himself as an illustrator, draughtsman, designer and inventor. He also studied the art of becoming a silversmith.

As the 1930s closed, he had established some profile in Sweden and seen his ideas published in magazines. He had also spent time in Paris studying sculpture and fine art in Paris just as Citroën's famed sculptor-designer Flaminio Bertoni was creating the Traction Avant and the early sketches for a streamlined replacement – the car that after the interruption of the Second World War, would become the Citroën DS.

Sixten Sason got himself a job working in the drawing and illustration office for Saab and there he would get noticed for his futuristic ideas and sketches of them. He provided early X-ray type see-through structural drawings and then sketched out styling ideas. In a 1941 design drawing, he shaped a Delta-configuration blended-wing type fighter jet with many futuristic motifs; argument still rages as to whether that design had any influence upon Saab's later Draken jet fighter so wonderfully designed by Erik Bratt.

As 1945 ended and 1946 dawned, Ljungström discussed car design with Sason and asked him to suggest some ideas for the shape of the first Saab car.

Ljungström said that as soon as he saw the strange, curved, aerodynamic wing- with wheels that was the sculpted form of the new Saab car design, he knew it was what they were looking for. It looked like a wing, but it had shades of French, Bohemian, and American design ideas in its wonderfully scaled form and stance. An upturned tortoise? A beetle? An insect? A frog? Or a flying saucer? Or perhaps some form of biomorphic device with wheels or indeed just a UFO born from 1940s aviation developments? Maybe 92 incorporate all these themes.

The Saab Board knew it was radical and nothing like any other car anywhere. With a smoothed-in one-piece 'pontoon' type body of monocoque type, this body shape was a huge gamble, one that went against the tide and had only been seen in stylistic terms in special racing car designs from Voisin and Bugatti. Perhaps the design works Lefebvre, Gerin, or Ledwinka and Jaray, might be part of Sason's inspiration (Porsche had yet to shape its 356), but the new car was radical departure indeed – as a first car from a company that had never made a car.

Low drag meant less fuel used, and the car was designed to be stable in terms of aerodynamic lift, and crosswind stability. The only real issue to solve were the covered wheel openings or shrouds – these had to be productionalised via a more rational approach.

Sason would go on to shape all the Saabs up to the first 99. He would design the Hasselblad cameras that went to the moon with the Apollo mission. He designed the Husqvarna Silver Arrow motorcycle, the first Electrolux vacuum cleaner, and a range of Swedish consumer product items – notably a wonderful waffle maker that looked like a spaceship from a 1950s American movie. But above all, he had created the domed, wing-hull style of the highly aerodynamic first Saab car. Sason thought in three dimensions and his Saab car design for the 92 was to prove timeless.

Rolf Mellde

As the car was developed into wooden styling model, then the first metal panelled prototype, a new name would join Saab in late 1946 fresh from Army service. This was Rolf Mellde. He had graduated from the Stockholm Institute Technical School, then he worked in marine engineering and also become a rally driver and motorcycle enthusiast. Mellde even came up with his own car design, but he joined Saab instead and brought a tenacious and forensic engineering and driving focus to the new car's development. Handling, steering, suspension and driving quality were all influenced by Mellde. Erik Carlsson developed the 92-96 series from the 1950s onwards, but the first Saab rally driver to influence and develop the 92 as a rally car and road car with relevant dynamics, was in fact Rolf Mellde. He also had Olle Landby inside the early Saab road test department – and he was a seasoned rally driver. Mellde organised the first rally entries of the new car in 1950 notably Swedish national rallies and the Monte Carlo Rally. In fact, Mellde won the 1950 Rikspokalen Rally in 1952 in the new 92. He also won the 1953 Swedish national rally championship. Of note, K.G. Svedburg had won the 1949 Tour of Ostgotland rally in new Saab 92. Mellde also drove with B. Carlqvist in 1950.

Female drivers took early Saab 92s to early 1950s rally successes and these names included: G. Molander, H, Lundberg, M. von Essen, and latterly U. Wirth, and E. Nystrom rallied a Saab with Pat Moss Carlsson.

For Saab's profile in America, B. Wehmann and L. Braun winning that year's Great American Mountain Rally, did a great deal of good.

Rolf Mellde developed the original Sonett, drove Saab's motorsport and engineering departments, urged Saab to seek a four-cylinder, four-stroke engine and he created Saab's first research department. We can credit him with making the 92 the driver's car that it was – and a rally and race car too. Many Saab fans will be familiar with 'Mellde's Monster' – the twin-engined x2-triple cylindered almost-V6 version of a Saab 93 that he developed as a one-off.

Engines were an area of focus for the 92, 93, and 96. From an initial transversely mounted two-stroke, two-cylinder in the 92, to the 1956 revision that was the 93 and its longitudinally mounted two-stroke valve-less three-cylinder engine, on to the 96V4's four-stroke, four-cylinder Ford-derived V4 engine.

Mellde was the force behind the development of the unique Sonett Mk1 and then the production versions that stemmed from its success.

Saab Rally & Erik Carlsson

Erik Hilding Carlsson became the legend of Saab and the driving and rallying of its cars. If you ever wondered how the 'feel' of the Saab car was created, look first to Rolf Mellde and then to Erik Carlsson. Erik developed the driving dynamics of Saabs right up to the early 1990s. Steering, brakes, gearbox, drivetrain and performance – all honed and shaped by Erik. Before that era, he was to become 'Mr Saab' as a global hallmark of the spirit of Saab and its cars.

Carlsson took the little Saab to great heights of rallying fame all over the world. He began riding Swedish, and British Norton motorcycles in the forests close to Trollhattan, then to practise 'rallying'. He worked for Per Nystrom the car dealers and had access to cars of differing types to practice on. Nystrom let Carlsson navigate for him in Nystrom's own rally car – a Volvo!

Carlsson then bought an early, second-hand Saab 92 and worked on it to improve its performance. He competed as a privateer in his Saab and soon Saab asked him in for chat. Rolf Mellde was instrumental in offering Carlsson help and in bringing him to Saab. A 'works' Saab drive soon followed (with Sten Helm as co-driver/navigator).

In 1954, Erik was an official Saab entry with no less a figure than Rolf Mellde as co-driver in a Saab 92 on the Masnatta Rally. Erik's first major championship win was in the Swedish Rikspokalen rally in a Saab 92 in 1955. He won the 10000 Lakes Rally in 1957 in a 93. In 1959 Erik and co-driver John Sprinzel paired up for the Rally of Portugal and came third.

Erik Carlsson won all the world's major rally events including the Monte Carlo Rally (twice) and every major title, except the East African Safari rally – in which he was podium placed several times but was thwarted to the victor's step. Carlsson won the RAC Rally three times in 1960, 1961, and 1962.

Stuart Turner was Carlsson's main British navigator/co-driver. John Brown and David Stone also paired with Erik in that role. Saab GB supplied support with Chris Partington being a youthful Saab support car driver. Gunnar Palm was one of Erik's closest mates and co-drivers in the cab; the pair won rallies all over the world. Torsten Aman was also often one of Erik's co-drivers in the glory days of a flying red Saab. Karl-Erik Svensson was also an Erik co-pilot as was Walter Karlsson – that pairing won the 1961 Acropolis Rally.

Erik won the 1962 Monte Carlo Rally with Gunnar Haggbom as his navigator/co-driver. 1963 saw G. Palm partner Erik and yet another Monte victory.

Ove Andersson was another Carlsson co-pilot in this era. In 1960, a privateer Saab 93 Sport driven by Carl-Otto Bremer/Eska Vainola also tackled the Monte.

Erik's wife Pat Moss Carlsson took many cars to rally fame – including the Saab 96 on the Ladies team. Her teammates in the car were Anne Riley, Ursula Wirth, and Elizabeth Nystrom. Pat and Anne also tackled the East African Safari Rally in 1962. Pat and Elizabeth were part of Saab's 1965 RAC Rally entry alongside Erik and Torsten. They had also entered in 1964 beside Erik and Gunnar.

However, prior to those events, Saab's late 1950s rally team had included Margareta von Essen, Monica Kjerstadius, Ewy Rosqvist, Helga Lundberg and Greta Molander. So women were always represented at the Saab rally team.

Other Saab rally team names that made the early cars their steeds included J. Sprinzel, W. Karlsson, T. Trana, E. Svensson, S. Nottrop, and G. Bengstsson.

In 1966, Erik rallied a Sonett II bored-out to 940cc with 92bhp. The car flew, as did Erik. But the Sonett was no 96.

After Erik Carlsson came the likes of Blomqvist, Cederberg, Eklund, Lampinen, Pettersson, Svensson, and many others, notably American drivers who rallied Saabs. We should not forget the rallying of the Saab 93-96 in South America in its heyday and of interest, in modern times. Key 1960s Uruguayan rally drivers with Saab 96 and 96 Sport cars included: Jose Arijon Hector Marcia Fojo, Torres de Oza; recent Saab 96 rallying in Uruguay and in Argentina was profiled by Carlos Abeiro with Juan Abeiro.

Erik Carlsson remained Mr Saab, a brand ambassador and even had a new Saab 9-3 Mk2 model variant named after him – has had been a classic 900Turbo with added 'Carlsson' stripes. Erik *was* Saab.

93 to 96

The twin-pot two-stroke 92 begat the three-pot two-stroke 93, and then there came a four-pot V4 from a Ford. Who knew in 1947 that this little car would get through three different engines and go from transverse engine layout to longitudinal in a sort of reverse-engineered genius so typical of Saab.

By 1955, Saab's first car had been modified, improved upon and regularly tweaked. The 92B (with a boot lid!) framed such improvements but still looked like the bluff-fronted launch model. Yet the company had learned much and also listened to Saab super salesman Philipson; they all knew Saab could revise the 92 into something more attractive on the global market. So 92 became 92B, then 93 by way of a lovely new nose job that Sason styled after yet another visit to Italy. Was that new front end influenced by Lancia or Alfa perhaps? Was a bit of (long-dead) French Voisin design language thrown in?

Launched on 1 December 1955 as a 1956 model year variant, the new 93 got a completely new nose, new suspension better heating and ventilation, 12volt electrics, new one-piece bumpers, a new gearbox design and many trim improvements. These were smaller changes than the big news – that being a new, German-derived engine design of three-cylinders (but still two-stroke cycle) was the highlight. A new, winter radiator blind that could be rolled down to keep Swedish snow and cold off the engine and also use a heater to warm the engine bay, was announced as the 'Klimator' device. The radiator was mounted behind the engine – not in front of it as per usual practice. Of note the new engine was still of front wheel-drive configuration but was longitudinally mounted.

Of 38bhp, the revvy, peppy new engine was from a Dr-Ing Hans Muller design and took its cue from earlier German engine developments of DKW and Heinkel ancestry. The engine's torque figure exceeded its bhp figure by quite a large percentage – always a sign of good engineering. Ljungström designed a new gearbox for the 93.

Coil springs and hydraulic dampers added greatly to the new car's ride quality.

The car was a success and a 93B debuted in 1958 with further specification improvements. A larger windscreen, more chrome trim, revised cabin and seats. Also in 1958, the 93 750 Gran Turismo model was launched. This was a sporty 93B with twin carburettors, 50bhp and a special rally-car tuning kit option that gave 57bhp (SAE) or 55bhp (DIN) if such varying measurement indices are required.

Extra seat padding, driving lamps, special badges, a three-spoke wooden steering wheel, new radial-type tyres and a revvy engine made this car a driver's favourite. It would also live on as the 750 GT Super – with further revisions.

Rattling along in that rasping flying saucer of car was a unique and wonderful sensation. It steered with the psychic precision of a Supermarine Spitfire, or maybe a Porsche 356.

By 1956, Saab had shipped its first export cars to America and the 93 had won an American rally (Great Mountain Rally of late 1956) and a factory-supported Carlsson was highly placed in the same event.

For 1959, the major changed was to be front-hinged doors to replace the old rear-hinged type. So the 93B became the 93F and also became even more internationally acceptable – despite its noisy and still smoky two-stroke engine. By 1960, an 850cc engine and significant trim and specification changes had created yet another iteration of the original late-1940s design origins. Saab-Sport and Saab Monte Carlo soon became badge-engineered marketing tweaks on either side of the Atlantic respectively. The new, forthcoming Saab 96 was the old bodyshell but with a revised rear window and side windows, new interiors, and here was another big stride for Saab. If only a four-stroke engine was readily available.

Meanwhile, the Saab 95 estate car arrived with 841cc and a four-speed gearbox (at last!) and of course the wonderful fold-down rear cargo cabin which could take a 500kg/1,100lb load. Announced in May 1959, actual production began in September of that year. But only 100 were built before Christmas. Early cars had a wonderful two-tone paint scheme. The 95 got the four-speed box before the 96, so Erik Carlsson drove a 95 in the Monte Carlo Rally, an estate car, rally car that was fourth in the Monte.

By late 1960, the new 96 with its heavily revised looks and much more deluxe cabin was on sale and making big strides for Saab in the global market. It had a drag co-efficient of CD.0.35 – very low indeed in age of an average CD figure being CD 0.50: By the 1970s, very few mass production cars got below CD 0.45. To Saab, such a high drag figure would have been deeply embarrassing in 1950, let alone 1980.

After several years of annual improvements to the 96 by Saab, the formula was beginning to show its limitations. But help was at hand and the 96 soon gained its licence-supplied Ford-sourced V4 engine and the car was transformed upon the road and on the rally stage.

Rolf Mellde was the driving force behind the move to four-cylinder power for the 96. He searched far and wide for a suitable engine; there had not been the money within Saab to design its own. Kjell Knutsson and Ingvar Andersson were Mellde's fellow engineers who set up a Saab engine research project, Paul Broman would lead the office as the team tried to find ways around the two-stroke mindset at Saab. Joseph Eklund led a series of experiments in this engine laboratory to refine combustion and emission qualities for the two-stroke Saab engine. But Saab's new engine would have to be quickly readied and easily inserted into the 96 without the need for major structural of dynamic re-engineering (new front wings and housings would however be required for the 96 V4). What about a compact little rotary of a V4 configuration? Possible engines included one from Lancia, or even Morris. But then came Ford with its tough, almost unburstable torquey, V4 as fitted to its newer range of mid-1960s cars.

The arrival of two-ex-Volvo engineers at Saab in 1964 – Olle Granlund and Per Gillbrand – ensured further engine knowledge was on hand. Rolf Mellde researched the Ford V4 and persuaded a top Saab figure (a Wallenberg family member), to pressure the Saab Board to invest in a new engine, not by design, but by borrowing one – from Ford. Via Detroit and Ford Germany, Ford agreed to a five-year licensing deal and soon, the V4 was fitted to the 96. Saab even briefly used Ford's own 'V4' badging on the 96 prior to a Saab-designed badge being ready. Early V4s were in fact two-stroke 96s with the old engines removed and the V4 added.

Saab modified the Ford V4, not least for extreme cold weather conditions engine and gave it softer valve springs, so it ran more smoothly. A lightweight fibre-constructed camshaft gear-wheel saved pennies and cost later problems with it. More power and more weight needed new brakes, and 96 got them via Lockheed with discs up front.

At 1498cc (1.5litres) and 73bhp (SAE), the car was faster through the gears and faster in top speed. Hard driving used fuel but gentle driving nudged 35mpg plus. The vital overtaking time from 30mph to 50mph was halved over the two-stroke's time of 20 seconds.

For the 1970s, and specifically for 1974, the 96V6 was given a heavy revamp with new interior, new seats, impact-bumpers (from 1975), vibrant colours, and more power at 1.7litres (from 1975). Saab's silver jubilee anniversary edition 96V4 was a deluxe trimmed version.

The British got a 'Souvenir' edition in late 1976. The later 96V4 Super, took the specification of the car about as far as it could go using a bodyshell originally designed before 1950. By 1978, 96V4 was Finnish built by Valmet and on the wane in terms of its sales appeal amongst more modern competitors. Saab needed a new small car to replace the icon, but it stepped in another direction.

Driving the early Saabs was an involving affair – the cars communicated back to the driver and the driver knew what the car was doing or would do next. The driver of an early Porsche 356 or a smaller Lancia might recognise this characteristic, as might the driver of an air-cooled Citroën. Minimal braking, plenty of stoking with the gearstick, and superb control from the direct and positive steering gave the conducting of these Saabs a wonderful feeling of mechanical engineering in action. Keep them on-the-cam, revved up, and the little Saabs, be they two-stroke or V4, simply flew. Saab had honed these cars to be driver's cars, yet cars that were safe, practical and fun: you could even install the 'bed' kit to your 93 or 96 and go camping in it.

The 96 lasted into the 1980s – just and at the end of production in 1980, Saab had sold 547,221 of its venerable 96 and 110,527 of its 95 estate car variant. A long-tailed hatchback version – the 98, was to be built only as a prototype. 96 had been built in various European plants, and we should not forget the knock-down kit-built 96-series cars built in Uruguay by Automotora Boreal of Montevideo. 378 of the 95 and 95 were built in Uruguay.

Sonett

Who built the world's first composite, alloy and resin-bodied lightweight sports car? Lotus? No. Saab!

Such was the original Sonett 1 – another Saab in the creation of which Rolf Mellde was instrumental.

Sonett was a secret project created by Mellde and a few Saab colleagues. It was designed, built and driven from a secret off-site location in a barn. These Saab men wanted a proper sports car with a Saab badge. Two-seat, open-topped in roadster style but using proprietary Saab engine and drivetrain components, the Saab 94, or Sonett as it became called (a name first dreamed up for a Saab in 1947 by Sixten Sason). Sonett derived from the Swedish 'Sa natt den ar' – meaning how neat is that. Sa natt was neat and so was Sonett or as we now term it, Sonett 1.

The glass fibre Saab Sonett coupés of the 1960s and 1970s that achieved production, were a different step from the ultra-lightweight sports-racer of 1954 that Mellde dreamed up for the original Sonett of Saab 94.

Aluminium and plastic panels were moulded and glued up to form a self-supporting body styled by Sason. No heavy iron or steel chassis was required. This hand-laid composite body weighed under 100kg/220lb. It was a stiff hull with aluminium side walls and curved, moulded outer skins. The body was built by a local boat building company from imported American glass fibre moulding and laying-up ingredients.

Key members of the team that made this secret little one-off included Rolf Mellde, Arne Frick, Lars-Olof Ollson, Olle Lindqvist, and Gosta Svensson. They built the car in a barn at a rural location half an hour's drive away from Trollhattan.

With a tuned-up 748cc three-cylinder two-stroke rasper of an engine under the bulkhead – as far back as possible for better weight distribution – and coil-spring suspension, the lightweight car was a true Special in the tradition of one-off cars. It was fast and could top 193kmh 120mph, was stiff, stylish and so much of a departure for Saab that it had to be unofficial.

Yet when Saab's management discovered the Sonett project, they let Mellde pursue it and then demanded that it be exhibited at the 1956 Stockholm, Motor Show.

Ultimately Saab would not take the first Sonett to series-production, yet six were to be funded and built by Saab sub-contractor ASJ in Linkoping and they employed a bodywork specialist concern called Karossverkstaderna, of Katrineholm. Sadly, the alloy and plastic mix had to be changed and the car's weight went over 600kg/1,1000lb, yet it was still a lightweight sportster and reaction, especially in America, was huge. If only it had had a four cylinder engine – that old Saab bugbear of the late 1950s rearing its head again.

Erik Carlsson raced the little 94 Sonett and won its debut race at Karlskoga races in 1957. Harald Kronegard and Clas Backström also raced the little car. Erik Lundgren won the 1957 Solvalla race in the car – with a faired-over passenger side of the open cabin. But Saab pulled the plug on the plans for Sonett 1 production.

Sonett 1 died. Saab briefly supported the Quantum single-seat racing cars of Walter Kern's idea in America, and then concentrated on development of the 96. But Sonett would return as the Sonet II and the fit for the 1970s, Sonett III. Both these cars would use steel Saab floorpans taken from the 95 and 96 parts-bin, Saab engines and of note, reinforced glass fibre bodyshells. As can be seen in the accompanying photographs and commentary, the Sonett lived on, a forgotten, two-seat, sporty Saab coupe sadly ignored except by the Saab cognoscenti and dedicated Saab 'geeks'.

Sonett II launched in 1966 via early production cars built in January of that year and took its cue from an idea for a Saab sportster designed as a concept by Björn Karlstrom as early as 1963. He built a glass fibre prototype with help from Malmo Flygindustri (MFI). Karlstrom's work became the Sonett II but produced by Saab and its glass fibre subcontractor ASJ. Somehow, some of Karlstrom's design's futurism had been diluted in the production iteration, yet here was a two- seat Saab sportscar. By late 1967, the car had been fully productionalised for the 1968 model year and soon you could order one with a triple-carburettor GT 850-type engine of 60 bhp. American versions used the lesser, 803cc engine with direct oil-injection seen in the 96 Shrike U.S. edition. Only 258 Sonett II were sold. However, drop the V4 engine from the 96V4 into the Sonett and what did you get – a much more sprightly sports Saab. This was not a Sonett II V4 but a stand-alone Sonett V4 with significant changes under the bonnet and in the structure.

Sonett V4 was heavier due that new engine, but cooler and smoother running, less frantic, and longer-legged. In 1969 a Sonett V4 driven b Simo Lapinen was third in its class in the Monte Carlo Rally. Over 1,500 Sonett IIs were sold up to late 1969.

Sonett III was born for the 1970s but did not use a body design by Björn Andreasson, and instead used a Sergio Coggiola. Saab's own Gunnar Sjögren finessed the details. Launched in 1970, Sonett III, early Sonetts wore rare and wonderful alloy wheels made by the Swedish company Tunaverken of Eskiltuna. Sadly, Saab decided to terminate this wheel option and use the 'football' style wheel design as often seen on the 96V4 and 99EMS.

America was the Sonett III's main market – notably from 1972 with the new 5mph-impact bumpers of cellular design taken from the 99 but shortened. With the new Saab corporate grille applied for the 1973 model year, Sonett III with the 1.7litre engine, wishbone-type front suspension and an internal roll cage, went well and felt taught. With a steel floorpan and Saab 96 and 95 engineering ingredients, this was no flimsy glass fibre bathtub. Larger bumpers, bigger tyres and wheels and extra trim took Sonett III to766kg/1,945lb by the time the car was phased out at the mid-point of the 1970s.

Sonett became an American favourite and Jack Lawrence tuned-up his Sonetts and went racing. Bruce Turk also became a Sonett guru amid the Sonett enthusiasts' niche. Turk made some interesting improvements to the car's track and wheel/tyre ratios to benefit the handling. From the early 1980s, the Vintage Saab Racing Group (VSRG) campaigned modified Sonetts and we saw privateer Sonett racing teams. George and Stefan Vapaa were well known Sonett saviours. Charles Christ, Randy Crook, Mary Anne Fieux, Steve Church, Ed Diehl, Chris Moberg, were all Sonnet campaigners.

Bud Clark became a major figure in 93, 96, and Sonett's tweaking and racing chapters of American Saabism. Tom Donney, the famous Saab driver and collector, took his Sonett II to race and record at Bonneville. John Jacobson also gave the 96 and the Sonett profile with various competitive drives.

Thanks to work at Saab in Sweden by Bo Hellborg in the Saab competition department and work on a mechanical fuel-injection unit for the V4 by Sigge Johansson, it was possible to get the engine to 165bhp, and in race tune 185bhp. Fit that to a lightweight Sonett III and the Saab would fly. But it did not *officially* happen and the injected V4 did not become a Saab 96 nor Sonett specification. However, fitting Weber carburettors from the official Saab Sport catalogue to the standard V4 engine also gave a performance boost. But Jack Lawrence would, over time, modify Sonetts with major 'blueprinting' to engine components, Solex carburettors, coated and polished parts and major re-workings of the combustion patterns and oil flow in the engine. These were expensive measures, but the serious Saabist wanted to exploit the V4 and the Sonett. He achieved major U.S. national titles with his tuned-up Sonett V4 in 1982 and even into the 1990s as Sport Light GT-4 champion.

So Sonett was a success albeit within its distinct Saab niche. Sonett across all its iterations represented a great Saab moment of free thinking and engineering, but as so often with Saab, the car was preaching to converted, not winning new conquest customers from other marques.

Left: This very rare piece is an original 1946 artwork by Sixten Sason as he was shaping the first Saab car. Perhaps old Sixten might have been a ladies' man – given how he often incorporated them in his car sketches. It was a shame that the faired-in front did not get through to production.

Below left: More futuristic Saab design from 1947 and another lady…

Below right: This Sason rendering is interesting because it shows the early prototype 92 in 1948 but with a 'Sonett' badge on the nose – circa 1947. So Sason (or Saab) thought of calling the 92 the Sonett way back then did he (or they)?

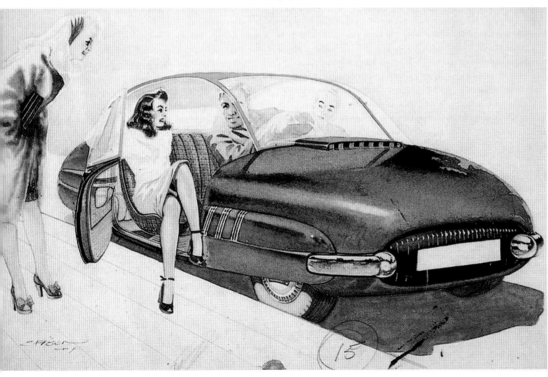

Right: Saab 92 X-Ray drawing from 1949 by Sixten Sason was used by Vastergtolands Museum in 2008 on their Sason exhibition poster. Note the Ljungstrom-engineered and aviation inspired structure and drilled panels.

Below: A 1936 car design by Sixten Sason – ten years before he shaped the Saab 92 'Vingprofil' Wing-profile car.

SIXTEN SASON

6/6 - 7/9 2008 Västergötlands museum
www.vastergotlandsmuseum.se 0511 26000 Skara

The early Saab 92 as created in a wood, clay, and black boot polished styling buck. This is the 1946 version, prior to the production-series frontal design. It is similar to the Sonett-badged rendering earlier.

1948 saw the 92.002 design proposal with a more conventional nose and light treatment take over from 92.001 and was a step closer to the production 92. This was in fact the third go at the front end design by Sason for Saab.

Scale Saab model with tuft testing in the Saab wind tunnel. Note how the airflow remained attached all the way along and down that quite steep tail – no Kamm-tail 'chop' being applied.

Another variation on the front-end design as 92.002. 1946 is the date on the Sason drawing and is a curious date as it pre-dates the styling of 92.001, with elliptical headlamps, the square-head-lamped Sonett-badged idea, and then the true 92.002 with tis round head lamps mounted high above a grille 'mouth'.

This 1938 sketch by Sason sees yet another amazing and futuristic car design and another lady – all in the best possible, politically-correct Swedish taste of course. Sason drew these designs years before the American 'space-ship' and aviation-inspired 1950s era of car styling. Is this where the idea of a UFO-of-a-car took route in his mind?

Left: Sason's exquisite badging for a car then un-named.

Below: URSaab seen in all its glory. Looking like a cross between a flying saucer, a Bugatti, a Tatra, and a Citroën then undreamed of, all added into a Saab design language ingredient: magic.

The men who made it happen for the Saab car: Left-to-right Svante Holm, Trygvve Holm, Gunnar Ljungstrom, Sixten Sason, Rolf Mellde. Heroes all.

Original Saab and the Saab 9-X of the early 2000s. Saab chief designer Michael Mauer seen when he led Saab design. Now he leads Porsche design. Oh what a fortunate man. Take a look at the 1947 URSaab 92.001 from the rear and then look at a Porsche Taycan's back end. Can you see anything familiar?

92.001 seen from the front with the shrouded wheels more obvious – subsequent changes were required to this aspect of the aerodynamic design.

A two-stroke engine and bits from DKW and Auto-Union are alleged to have been used to build the prototype 92.001.

The stunning sculpture and scaling of Sason's 92.001 are captured in this view of the spaceship that became a Saab. Is there a touch of Komenda's 1930s Porsche fastback styling in there? Fast-forward and a feel of Saab-Porsche language is discernible.

Above: An original Saab publicity shot of a lovely maroon 92 and that is a Saab boat (designed by Kurt Sjögren, Sixten Sason and the Saab team) can be seen on the water behind. The sheer character of the 92 shines through in this lovely old photograph.

Right: Australian Saabist Henk Ossendrijver took this great picture of his West Australian-registered 92B in a stunning tropical WA setting. The sun shone on Saabs down under and many still populate the outback

92B (1955) owned by Saab expert Ken Dover. This car appeared in the *Top Gear* Saab tribute episode, and had also appeared on Top Gear decades earlier. In the UK, Sam Glover, the motoring writer at *Practical Classics,* has recently added his 92 production car to the British stable of three UK-registered 92s. At one time in fairly recent history there were six 92s on UK roads. Martin Healey's chassis 009 as one of the first of the twenty final design pre-production prototype 92's being a highlight. Chris Hull's collection of 92s and 93s underline the brilliance of these cars and their modern owner's enthusiasm.

Left: Here, the details show off Sason's forensic design work in the door handles. This was design purism and set the standard for Saab engineering forensics.

Below: 92B (with opening boot lid to identify it over the 92 that did not have an opening boot) seen in company with the two-stroke Sonett Mk2.

A lovely Saab photograph of a green 92 hustling along a Swedish road in the summer. Can't you just hear that ringa-ding-ding buzz from the twin-pot engine?

Above and right: Saab 93 GT750 legend. Note the badging, roof-light and curved scaling.

Chris Hull's lovely 93B 773 XUR was expertly tuned by ace Saabist Graham Macdonald. Hull now owns several early 92s and 93s. Such is the Saab 'infection' – that leads us to the 'Saab Shop'. Is there not something obviously 1930s French-German aerodyne-streamliner about the 92-93 cars' swooping style? Chris owns the 92B that resided in Casablanca as an ex-French Saab in Africa. What stories these cars can tell. Imagine meeting a 92 scything along a north African road!

Right: 96, the masterstroke from 'Sixties: the '500 KNX' two-stroke of Mike and Norma Thompson is a well-known and much loved Toreador Red Saab with the 'Italian' front styling by Sason – or 'bullnose' as some call it; if you have too…

Below: The legend on a chassis plate 'SVENSKA AEROPLAN AKTIEBOLAGET' of Linkoping, Trollhattan, Sweden.

Below: Erik Carlsson's replica car headed the red Saab convoy at Erik's memorial service. The car marked the win on the 1960 RAC Rally by Carlsson and Turner. With three RAC rally victories and two Monte Carlo Rally wins, two-stroke power never had it so good. Few beyond the Saab circle know of the Saab '60' – a special Saab 96 built between June 1962 to April 1963 as a one-off edition of 56 cars of special trim based upon a revised engine of 60hp via a new crankshaft, sports-flow exhaust and with lowered suspension. This car was an Erik Carlsson Monte Carlo Tribute that stood in for the Saab Sport models seen elsewhere.

Above: Another Saab legend – Chris Partington, Saab tuner and modifier and former Saab GB stalwart (ultimately as Technical Director) and rally support driver at the height of the rally years. Seen here with LDH 781D his Le Mans Classic, 'Sarthe – Stroker' as a 93B special that he created to take a Saab to Le Mans in 2010, where once such Saabs competed in an age past dated 1959 when two 93s were entered in the 24 hours Le Mans race. It was Syd Hurrell and Roy North who entered and drove their private 1959 entry, a green-hued 93: Saab also entered one (grey) 93 as well. More recently Chris Partington, Chris Parkes and Chris Nutt took their green replica of that 1959 private entry Saab to the 2010 Le Mans Classic. The 748cc Saab topped 100mph on its two-stroke mix of oil, smell, smoke, and that wonderful, even primordial sound. The 'Saabisti' – Saab fans suffering from Saabism, and Saabitis, loved the sight and sound of LDH doing its stuff. Motoring journalist John Simister tracked Chris and the car to France and back in his own 96.

Above: The Carlsson memorial service line-up of red Saabs: Saab emotion.

Right: Mike Thompson's 500KNX was a fitting tail-end Charlie to the Carlsson tribute.

David Lowe's 1964 Saab 96 two-stroke of longitudinal layout three-cylinder (an engine of Heinkel, Muller, Eklund engineering provenance) is a wonderful non-original original. Mechanically modified using real Saab parts by a certain Mr Partington during his prior ownership tenure, the car reeks of Saabism and the smell of Saab. David blasts the stroker around West Country lanes in blur of Saab style. The original interior is a purist's joy. Don't clean it David.

You can argue that you prefer the round instrument dials of earlier versions, but you cannot argue with the utter originality of 24 NPO's cabin. Here lies more than patina, but the psychometry of a car and its life and its driving. A nice, original pot of Saab two-stroke oil mix additive somehow adds to the moment and the memory. Only an insensitive soul would wipe all this originality out to replace it with new everything of plastic provenance. David is keeping the car original.

Above: Saab – the legend stylised by Sason's brilliant new front end design for late 1956 onwards on the 93. He called it the 'Italian front' as it aped Lancia, and Alfa Romeo motifs: was there a bit of pre-war Voisin thrown in too? Adding the 'Aeroplan' aircraft logo just seems so right. The new frontal design remained the face of the subsequent 96 model from 1960 onwards until the 'long-nose' design appeared on the 95 and the 96 from 1965 onwards.

Left: Two-tone blue for the two-stroke talisman. These were proper car seats designed for long distance and rally use. This is originality – and must never be 'restored' to 'pebble bleach' standards of wiping out history to be so-called better than new, and devoid of history. This is a real car, not an over-restored 'replica'.

Saab expert Chris Partington at the wheel of 24 NPO – as captured by the author riding in the back. We were stroking along at full warp speed.

A late 1961 Saab 96 with the rare Fichtel & Sachs Sax-o-mat automatic centrifugal clutch mechanism linked to engine speed via throttle position with electro-mechanical operation via a servo clutch with gear lever activation by touch – first launched on the 93 of 1957. Of often ignored note, the fitting of the Sax-o-mat created changes in the engine configuration – a fact that makes mechanical restoration more testing today. DKW had been the main user of the Sax-o-mat (also Borgward, Opel, Fiat, and VW), and Saab took it up for the late 1950s. A small number of such Saabs were sold with DKW-sourced Sax-o-mat badging. WSU 248 is seen speeding along with owner Arthur Civill at the helm.

Inside WSU 248 with left hand-drive plus Sax-o-mat. Sheer style. Arthur's car is unique in the UK and was previously owned by dedicated Saabist Chris Hull (Hull owned the 93 'XUR'). Very few original Sax-o-mat cars remain even in Sweden.

The post-1956 classic Italian-style frontal restyle worked well with the later domed roof and the enlarged rear side windows of the later 93 that became the 96 from 1960 onwards. The three cylinder engine, revised interior, new trim specifications and of course the Sax-o-mat gearchange all created a virtually 'new' car for Saab – latterly to receive the V4 engine. From 1962, full, three-point seatbelts in the front were standard fittings. Arthur Civill's very rare car poses in front of Cadbury Castle in Somerset. Along with the Sport and GT models, this is the type of 96 which has become a rapidly appreciating asset and might soon top £25,000 on a good day at the right auction to the right person.

Three-pot perfection in detail: the Swedish (Eklund-engineered) engine of German provenance via, By late 1965, a new nose and a triple-carburettor version with more power and less oil required in the petrol mix had arrived.

Round dial speedometer rather than a strip-type device offered a more classic design element to the newer dashboard of the mid-1960s. A wood-rimmed steering wheel also looked good on the Sport, GT and Monte Carlo editions. Interestingly, this car has the later single-dial, not the twin-dial set up. In certain markets, notably Switzerland and the U.S., a hybridised 'Special' trim specification saw the separately lubricated 55hp engine of the Monte Carlo 850 (Saab Sport outside the U.S.) model.

Above: These two green dream machines are later 96s from the 1970s. The car on the right (WGU) owned now by Jim Keniston, is a car known to some as 'Mavis' (once painted beige) and has had an earlier nose panel and round headlamp panel (first launched in late 1965) retrospectively added by its previous restorer Ian. The reader can decide which front end looks better: beauty being in the eye of the beholder. Taking the spot-lamps off let more air into the engine bay, resulted in cooler-running. With black-painted 'elephant's ears' rear air vents, 'soccer' type alloy wheels, a fresh interior and much mechanical fettling, this is a super Saab for sure.

Left: The famous 'Soccer' football type Saab alloy wheel design seen in detail. Rarely seen without the black-painted sections, the wheel looks very good in one-colour finish without the black sections.

Saab 95 estate two-stroke being Ian Meakin's car, first registered in the UK in December 1966. Looking utterly classic in slate grey rather than a snazzy two-tone paint job sometimes seen on 95 estates. Saab's first estate car was launched in 1959 for the 1960 model year. Only 55 of these estate cars (with rear-hinged front doors) were built in 1959, prior to full availability from 1960 onwards. 95 was to receive the first Saab four-speed gearbox and Erik Carlsson drove one in the Monte Carlo Rally.

Above: Simon's Saab 'SDV' shows off its face in an earlier paint scheme – using the word advisably. So Saab.

Top left: The 95 sports a Saab loo roll under a Saab wooden steering wheel (Mota Lita of course) – real Swedish style then…

Left: This early 1964 seems to be happy in the sunshine: those spot lamps seem to add to the moment. Note the twin side strips. This beastie is of course the rare GT850 model – fully renovated and very much on the go. She spooled up and rasped away as a stroker should. Is that Neil at the wheel?

Green greatness: Ron van Heeswijk sprints away at the wheel of his lovely 96V4. Somehow those rectangular lights look right in this setting – minus the rubber bumper of course.

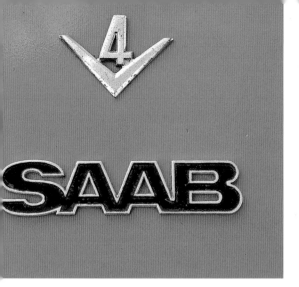

Above: Non-standard Saab delights: the later Saab logo badge seen below the curious and rare V4 badge as briefly used on the early production run V4s. This was a Ford Europe-sourced V4 badge which went with the Saab's Ford V4 engine –until Saab came up with its own V4 badge. Mounted high on the 96 front wing, these badges are now a rarity.

Right: It is 'SDV' again – and why not because she looks so right. White wall tyres and patina. Saabtastic – unless you are a purist of course… I am not.

Left: Oily rag is fantastic. Seen at Prescott Hill Climb, SDV 188N just keeps on giving. The roof 'slicer' looks great and get the tarp over the ute section. Outback delight. Saab missed a trick with this one. 95 van spec was one thing, but the ute looks so good. Originally built by Roger, now looked after by Simon.

Left: A corner of Bruce Turk's fantastic 'Saab barn' in the USA. Here the top, old-Saab enthusiast and restorer fettles his collection of Saabs. He drives the blue 96 two-stroke with the verve and style of a Swedish rally ace.

Below left and below right: Classic 95 in a colour redolent of its era – as the 1970s dawned. This 1971 95 (owned by Chris Boffey) was the subject of a major restoration to superb standard; it has the larger windscreen and updated trims of its model year. By 1971 the chrome strips over each wheel arch had gone. The mud flaps are more like snow-slicers. Finnish-built 95s and 96s were well made, and beautifully painted. This was also the year that the 1.7-ltire V4 was sold in America. This car captures a certain Saab aura of the era ...

Saab 96 fastback and Saab 95 flatback: guess which one is more aerodynamic?

867 GLO with sports stripes, spoiler, Minilite-type wheels, a roll cage and blue paint. That rubber lip spoiler low on the boot lid was wind tunnel-designed by Saab and actually aided airflow separation and vortex control despite being low down on the tail. Super Saab.

A selection of Saabs: evolving design language captured off the rear of a classic 900.

Opposite: Haa haa! HAA 138K is the lovely 1974, 95 van project. Pure blue Svenska.

Above and opposite: Chris Redmond's wonderful 1963, 96 'stroker' in all its patina and presence. Chris previously restored a 95 estate and a classic 900. A dedicated Saabist, he now makes a major commitment to the running of the British, Saab Owners Club. His 96 complete with leather bonnet strap, number decals, and raising power simply reeks of Saabism.

The real thing – clean but original. Thank goodness for that. This cabin tells its own story.

Right: Now, it might be non-original, but BCV 96K is a wonderful amalgamation of Saab motifs. Behind is the privately built 96 cabriolet.

Below left: This is 'Cabotine', Jean Francois Bouvard's (who took the photo) self-built 96 open tourer cabriolet seen in the French Alps. Note the reinforced windscreen frame. Extra side fillet panels above the sills added lost rigidity after the removal of the roof: sheer joy.

Below right: The face of Saab – putting light on the subject. An orange dream.

Saab snout. Enough said.

This wonderfully evocative 96V4 Souvenir Edition belongs to Saab Owners Club stalwart Mike Philpott - who chaired the club for years. Mike and his son Alistair have owned and restored dozens of old Saabs and are true Saabists. This car is Nr.122 from the batch of 150 final 96V4s that Saab GB sold from its key British base. Saab GB was set up by retired RAF Squadron Leader Robert Moore DFC and Bar who, post-war, became a Saab test pilot in Sweden and flew the Saab J29 Tunnan prior to importing his own Saab 92 and then setting up Saab's hugely successful British operation as the 1960s dawned. It was Moore who who promoted Saab by getting famous names to drive the cars: Such celebrities included Jackie Pallo, Raymond Baxter, Eric Morecambe, and Ernie Wise. Moore roped in Stirling Moss - as Erik Carlsson's wife's brother. Moore was hugely respected and flew his own Saab Safir monoplane in air races accompanied by his wife Georgie.

The original 'real' Sonett of 1956-1957, latterly seen with Erik at the wheel. The registration SAAB 94 is of course entirely accurate.

Left: Sonett as production Sonett MkII seen in the original Saab photograph from 1967. A glass fibre and steel hybrid composite Saab two-seater designed by Bjorn Karlstrom and stemming from marine ply, steel, glass fibre and Malmo Flygindustri – hence the code of 'MFI', all amid the entrails of Sason's earlier coupé idea seen in his 'Catherina' prototype.

Opposite: NAL 349E is a famous 1967 early-build Sonett Mk II two-stroke, owned and expertly driven by Peter Briggs. One of only 258 ever manufactured and with the original bonnet hump moulding – not the larger, curved V4 hump.

NAL 349E has the earlier wooden dashboard: rarity value.

Opposite: The same car coming down the Prescott hill. Sonett's are very special indeed to the Saab purist.

The Sonett sensation: David Barrow's 1967 Sonett MkII MKD 106E hares down Prescott Hill. Two-stroke power, or V4 1.5 for the Sonett II, but never V4 1.7 it seems.

V4 with modifications to get it in under that low-line glass fibre bonnet.

The Sports cockpit of the Sonett III. One-piece moulded seat pans were years ahead of the mainstream car makers and debuted in the 1966 Sonett II.

Late 1972 Sonett III of Sergio Coggiola design provenance and Gunnar Sjogren design input. This is an original long-nosed in Burnt Orange and not defaced with the later cellular impact-bumpers which were taken from the revised 99, cut down, re-joined and fitted to later Sonett IIIs. Typical Saab ... This December 1972 car has the SAAB side-stripes of the 1973 cars but not the big bumpers. Introduced in 1970, Sonett III was revised by Saab up to 1974 and last chassis 97745002483 – which even had headlamp wipers on the pop-up lamps as seen on the last series cars.

Super Sonett design included the sliced Kamm-back and rear glass hatch. Saab's pert little sportster looked great in 1970s orange too.

Above: The green car is an impact-bumper Sonett III and the gold car is the well-known two-stroke Sonett II.

Left: Saab yellow – or Mellow Yellow as they called it. Seen on a Sonett with the extra lamps hidden behind the grille.

Of salt and Saabs: Famed American SaabistTom Donney's modified Sonett II 750cc class car hit 122mph at Bonneville in 2012 and then got to 123.885mph in 2016 for a new record. The needle went over 124mph at one stage. Tom handed the drive over to Steve Myers who proved the concept. In 2018, Tom got the Sonett to 130mph with an average of 128.7mph. That is over 100mph in third gear! Dan Haugh of Kansas ran a classic 900 at the same Bonneville meet and hit 142.095mph. Back in 1963 Dick Catron took a Saab 93 two-stroke (with a tuned Saab Motors USA engine via Bob Wehman's help), to a new class record at 98.079mph at Bonneville. Catron owned the Saab dealership in Denver – which might have been helpful… Catron actually got the 93 to 101.99mph with a tailwind component. In 1964, Catron went back to Bonneville with a 93F and a Saab 940cc engine tuned up by Rolf Mellde and got the car to 105.453mph. Tom has set up his Saab museum to global appreciation,

Sonett sensation – the original 1950s Sonett as seen in an official Saab photograph.

Left: Joel Durand is a leading light of the French Saab Club and this is his photograph of his lovely Sonett (II) V4 in a non-factory but very attractive colour scheme. The car is parked over the Sonnette River in the Charente region of south west France! You can see the different front bonnet moulding 'bulge' to cover the V4 engine installation in a car originally offered as two-stroke in very low production numbers (230). Sonett V4 came in in late 1967 and almost touched the next decade.

Below: Seen from another angle, Joel Durand's Saab Sonett V4 displays its pretty rump and glazed rear window 'hayon bulle' design. 1,610 Sonett (II) V4 were produced before the Sonett III took over in 1970. Sonett V4 made an excellent road and track racer in the USA.

Right: A Saab press shot of Erik Carlsson hassling the Sonett II (2-stroke) on a Swedish dirt road as only Erik could: an old photo but an atmospheric and evocative one.

Below: Bjorn Cederberg in the 96 V4 rally car captured at speed in a Saab press photo. Real Saab action from the heyday.

This two-stroke 96 beauty is captured as she enters the car park of ANA the Saab dealer in Trollhättan. Two keen Saabists across the generations are inside the super Saab cabin. A Saab on Swedish plates in Sweden captured by Robin Morley of 'Swedish Day UK' fame.

Saab 93 with front-opening doors – so it's an early one. A lovely blue hue and with Saab Sport accessories fitted too. For Saab purists, this one is the real deal: sheer joy as captured in Sweden by Robin Morley.

2

99: Stylish Swede

99 Turbo rally car with the right decals and American-spec headlamps. Saab Dealer Team specification looked like this.

As the 1960s evolved, change was in the air for car manufacturers. Incredibly, if we look beyond the Citroen DS, the NSU Ro80, the Rover P6 and one or two other types, car design remained in a world of iron blocks, boxy bodies, rear wheel-drive, leaf-spring suspension, scant attention to safety or aerodynamics, and lowest common denominator school of engineering and design.

The likes of Ford, GM, Chrysler, VW, Fiat, Renault, etcetera, and eventually the Japanese manufacturers, set the standard of what they thought the customer wanted and what the car maker could offer as a prescribed formula. Vinyl roofs, sports wheels, bigger engines, fuel injection, side stripes, headrests, chrome embellishments, fast facelifts and old cars re-skinned into so-called 'new' cars, this was the game that was played upon the car buyer who though that he or she was getting the state of the art – but was not. The big car makers churned out the mundane. In the late 1970s, the likes of VW, Alfa Romeo, and Citroën, offered a little more via the new VW Golf and the AlfaSud, and the GS, respectively. But in the mainstream, cast iron, tarted-up tin steel and vinyl was the order of the prescribed marketing day.

Saab would have none of it.

The 99 was a consumer design of durable delight that offered the very highest levels of cabin strength and safety, good airflow details, and many new aspects of engineering for mid-range car.

From 1964 to 1967, 'Project F' was framed – the bigger Saab that would take the company to a wider market. It was better known as 'Project Gudmund' after the date it was born in the Swedish calendar.

Designed by Sixten Sason in his fading days of health, finessed by a young Björn Envall and then reinvigorated by him in its later 1970s editions, Saab's late-1960s 99 was a car with much to offer that was innovative and rewarding.

Originally sketched by Sason on spare notepaper from the Hotel Bele in Trollhattan, the 99 had a distinctive concave, swept rear end and C-pillar, and a highly curved front windscreen as its original design elements. Aribert Vahlenbreder, Ralph Johnson and then a young Björn Envall were to contribute to the final shaping of the 99's sculpture. Henrik Gustavsson was the 99's technical project director.

The car had an aerodynamic drag coefficient of CD of 0.37 when most of its rivals were struggling to get down to CD 0.44.

Over four years, the new two-door car, to be tagged '99' was engineered to the highest standards. Thick metal, the strongest, heaviest metal-gauge windscreen pillars ever fitted to a mass-production car, fronted a reinforced cabin and very strong roof. A British, Triumph/Ricardo originated engine design was sourced under licence and then Saabised.

Front-drive, expensive front double wishbone and multi-link rear suspension with coil springs, dampers and a Panhard locating rod at the rear, all gave the 99 its sure-footed handling and good ride quality. Very few car makers fitted double wishbone front suspension to mainstream family cars at this time.

The Saabist knows that with its new car, the 99, Saab side-stepped such self-limiting convention and offered its customers something more, a car that was truly new, a car that offered better safety, better seat comfort, better driving and dynamic behaviour, and a distinct Swedish design language which nevertheless would appeal beyond the Baltic to a global fan base.

Launched with steel 'chrome' finish bumpers and 1960s-type trim, the 99 was advanced but perhaps dated in its trimmings due to its long gestation period that included a year of test-development driving with approved and chosen customers. The bumpers, trims, brightwork and seats and cabin were quickly to be updated for the 1970s.

Three-people could sit across the rear seat; the front seats were strong and expertly designed. You could also fold the back seat down and load cargo through from the boot, or even sleep in the car – just as you had been able to do with the 96.

Thick paint, thick rustproofing, PVC-coated brightwork, durable cabin materials, and an air of quality added to the mix and made the 99 a truly wonderful Saab.

The four-door arrived in 1970 and the heavy styling revision of under Envall's brilliant pen effectively reinvented the 99 as a 'new' car for the 1970s. In 1972, there then came the injected EMS sports version which was delight to drive and opened up a new road that led to the 99 Turbo and all that implied for Saab, not just for the car. By 1974, EMS was a near- 120bhp car. Here was a car to compete with the new range of faster, upmarket BMWs.

1973 gave us the three-door 99 with its elegantly swept elongated tail and hatchback – more Envall design brilliance that just reeked of Saab and 'aero' design and yet which established a new design language for the company.

Increasing focus on side-impact issues led Saab to lead the world by adding to the 99s reinforced doors by fitting steel anti-intrusion bars incorporated into the frame, and a special interior door panel that offered smooth contours and energy absorbing materials to avoid impact with the occupants' ribcages.

Special steel fillets were added to the box section under-sill panels and door apertures. 99 exceeded all known crash legislation and did so for decades. Its torsional rigidity approached 6,000 lb/ft/degree – less than the original Saab 92 with its sealed up hull, but double the stiffness rating of most contemporary cars to the 99 in the 1970s. 99 resisted twist by more than 30 per cent higher than its competitors. You could drop a 99 on its roof from eight feet high and the roof would stay upright and the doors open.

Olle Lindqvist, Lars Nilsson and then Christer Nilsson were the key names of the 99's structural safety advances. Saab's 99 won the 1972 Don Safety

Trophy for delivering what the Don Safety Committee called 'the most remarkable safety package'. Esteemed editor of *Car* magazine, Mel Nichols, stated that the 99's strength and safety was of significance.

But 99 was not just passively crash-safe, it had active safety – it drove and behaved superbly. Erik Carlsson test-developed the car and ensured that it drove and felt like a Saab – a car that tells the driver what is happening. Heavy, unassisted slow-speed steering was to be the 99's only real issue in terms of dynamics.

The iron-blocked, alloy-headed engine was tough and even tougher in Saab specification under Saab engineer Per Gillbrand's expertise; the engine was ripe for development. Putting power through the gearbox and front drive mechanism would require development, especially under the turbocharged specification that 99 adopted.

At 1709cc and 85bhp this was a good all-purpose engine, and soon it would grow to 1894cc, then 1985cc and 110bhp, 99 would have real performance, especially with fuel injection.

Turbo Induction

Per Gilbrand led the development of the 99 Turbo – the world's first practical and reliable application of turbocharging to a mass market car. This turbocharger unit was no bolt-on quick trick, it was carefully engineered into a revised engine and cylinder head and properly tested to prove its reliability. A revised camshaft, stronger valves, different metals and qualities inside the cylinder head were all focused upon. A safety valve or waste-gate to 'dump' excess internal turbocharger pressure proved to be key to reliability.

In the 99 Turbo, torque was up 45 per cent, power up by 23 per cent. Torque was 245Nm/kg/175lb/ft – nicely exceeding the 145bhp total engine power rating.

Ex-Scania engineer Bengt Gadefelt brought turbocharging knowledge to the project amid Joseph Eklund, Karl-Erik Peterson, and British consultant Geoffrey Kershaw, all of whom engineered the 99's turbocharger into reality. Sten Wenlo was the Saab director who led the Saab management decision to go for turbocharging. Wenlo literally was the driving force behind the Saab 99 Turbo era.

The key team on the creation of the 900 were: Stig Norlin as head of 900 project development; Björn Envall as chief designer; Harry Erikson as interior designer; Bernt-Ake Karlsson as design modelmaker; Richard Olsson body engineering; Lars Nilsson as safety expert; Hakan Danielsson as aerodynamicist; Olle Granlund as engine and turbo expert; and Magnus Roland running test and development.

Spool-up lag was of course a turbocharging problem, but Saab put an immense number of hours in to trying to reduce this inherent mechanical problem of turbocharging. Below 2,000 rpm, the engine was as normal, but after that, turbo-pressure built as the exhaust-flow driven 'windmill' spun faster and faster to increase local pressure into the combustion process. Over the ensuing years, Saab would continue to develop the turbo application and evolve its characteristics and emissions.

99 Turbo overtook with sensational urge, it had near-supercar performance and yet the torque-curve was not too peaky and the soundtrack was wonderful. The turbocharger had smoothed out the noise harmonics of the exhaust and the cylinder head, the engine was no heavy-breathing valve-bouncer. Saab had achieved a miracle of engineering.

Driving the 99 Turbo was astounding. The car was transformed into a real flyer. Dropping a gear and synchronising the application of throttle to the slight turbo-lag, and the road conditions, quickly delivered a true rocket-ship rush headlong up the road with minimal steering tug, nor torque-steer. Through the shallow, curved windscreen, the road zoomed towards you as the whistling sound of turbo-motoring manifested. Driver and occupants were pushed back into their seats and thrust truly was felt. Being careful with the gearbox and making deliberate, paced, gear-changes could extend gearbox life in the 99 Turbo. The car was a driving sensation and hype did not need to be descriptively applied.

This early Saab turbocharging application would be a major chapter in Saab's history and one that was industry-leading. From it would become the Saab low-pressure turbocharger (LPT) application and the evolution of the 99 into the more up-market 900.

This sketch by Sixten Sason was made in the early 1960s and showed themes of the 99 allied to a smaller size and aerodynamic nose as a potential new small Saab. Note the Delta-wing Concorde-like motif in the background – although Concorde came along long after Sason's death.

This 1970-registred original Sason-designed 99 shows off its 1960s modernity and shiny steel bumpers (sometimes cited as 'chrome'). All the bright trim was stainless steel encased in plastic film – real Saab quality. 99 was designed and tooled by 1996, tested for over a year and long-gestated prior to its 1969 main launch with the 'base' 1.7-litre engine and a clock from the 96 on the dashboard.

The revised Envall-designed 99 update transformed the car at minimal expense but greatest impact. Note the impact-bumpers and front spoiler. Inside was completely new fascia moulding and trim design.

EMS – fuel injection sport trim 99 with the 99's second (larger) 1.85litre 95hp engine replaced with a 1,985cc (injected) engine of more direct Saab design over the old Triumph-Ricardo engine's roots. This new engine with numerous improvements delivered the EMS 110hp. EMS came in Copper Coral Metallic and had special badging.

The rare sight of three EMS in varying specifications.

EMS coming around the bend at Prescott.

Above: This EMS has the revised grille motif of 1975 and 118hp due to revised fuel injection. EMS was and remains a much underestimated 99 that was sadly eclipsed by the Turbo.

Right: It might not be factory-spec but this EMS with its stripes and spoilers is certainly effective.

Above left and above right: Very hot! Under the hood of the 99T rally car.

Left: The author's Saab hero – Stig Blomqvist with a 99 Turbo at the height of his and its fame. Note the wheel arch extensions and how the rubber bumpers have deformed behind the spot lamps.

Above left: The Saab-Sason curve of the original two-door 99 captured.

Above right: David Dallimore's wonderful, award-winning 99 Turbo restoration photographed from a low angle captures the essential 99 design language. David is a dedicated Saabist and he and his car are part of Great Western Saabs in England's West Country.

Right: David's car catches the light on its taught sculpted panel work. The rising line was even more obvious in the three-door 99 bodyshell as opposed to this two-door version.

Above and opposite: Passing the camera, 99 Turbo on the move with the Inca wheels spinning and light falling on those expertly scaled panels.

Above: Inca architecture framed. Alloy wheel design as a Saab speciality.

Left: The stunning interior of the Turbo branding. That steering wheel was lovely. Apparently the new seat for the 99 was designed by a Mr Berglof.

Above left: Acacia Green from 1979 was a more subtle colour for the Turbo.

Above right: Red Turbo with the four round headlamps of the U.S. specification and the 99 'Airflow' body kit.

99s under the sun: 99 had a friendly 'face' and somehow the square headlamps looked just right.

Opposite: Under the Turbo bonnet. Note the 'TURBO' branding as cast.

Right and below: This 99 Turbo sports the unusual Saab 99 body kit and rear spoiler accessory and two-tone paint in a French setting with owner Alain Rosset at the wheel in Bretagne.

Above: Under the bonnet of the 99. Saab slant-head nicely fettled.

Opposite above: The four-door 99 came along in 1970 but this one is a 1980s car with various trims items from the 900 model range that were grafted onto the later 99s.

Opposite below: Beige but lovely. An interestingly trimmed 99 with early-model mirrors, wheels from the 900 range, round headlamps and a sunroof.

Above and opposite: Alan Sutcliffe was a dedicated Saabist and after a 96 restoration, his 99 automatic in white with Turbo wheels looked very modern indeed for a mid-1960s car design. Saab – timeless beyond fashion.

Left: The 99 three-door was an elegant Envall revision to 99. This unusual angle captures the aerodynamically shaped rear hatch shaping. '99GL super' meant what it said.

Below: This 90 was fitted with a larger engine of Turbo specification and featured numerous upgrades from TR Autos of Yeovil whose proprietor is a well-known Saab owner and restorer. In fact, it sports a Turbo16v engine, the DI kit, and running gear from a 900 and some interesting parts added, including water-injection. Mastering the art of the steering might have been required. The car has a unique and bespoke interior.

3

900: Classic Saab

900 was a new car but because it was partly based upon the underpinnings of the old 99, some critics failed to 'get' what the 900 did.

This new car was no facelift, instead it was a fundamental re-engineering of the 99 and this included a longer wheelbase, a new front end, major structural and engineering revisions and a new style for Saab. 900 was a bigger car – taking Saab into the executive class, and in the 900 Turbo and 16 Valve Turbo, real performance car territory.

Like 99, 900 had a true feel for the road and was a responsive driver's car that contained the legacy of Saab's origins and its men. 900 was a tactile drive yet also one of quality and class.

Launched in Monte Carlo, the 900 debuted in black with unusually-styled 'Inca' type alloy wheels, new Michelin tyres, crimson velour interior trim and de-chroming to the brightwork. With its long-nose, 'flat-front', sweeping curves and wonderful attention to detail, the new 900, even as base-model trimmed with brightwork and hubcaps, was a very serious car indeed.

This car was indeed, as Saab claimed, one of the most thoroughly and carefully engineered cars on the market in the 1980s. Like Porsche, Saab added constant revisions to engines, seats, styling (the slant-front was seen on later cars) to each model year development as continuous improvement to an already fantastic package.

With a longer-wheelbase, revised suspension and improved tyre technology, the 900 rode and drove with top quality characteristics. The 900 Turbo was a legend amongst Saab owners, but the injection and carburettor models were sold, dependable, long-lasting cars that families took their hearts. From three-door and five-door at launch, to a soft-top convertible, then a four-door saloon with a distinctive new rear boot-line, to the later, two-door saloon, 900 evolved. Saab sold over a million 900s including 48,888 of the stunning convertible. Over twenty special editions were marketed either via Saab or via dealer editions: also seen were the special bodykit 'Aero' or 'SPG' cars, and the fully-equipped Carlsson models.

As for driving the classic 900 Turbo and its drive, well, that surge of turbo-forced thrust, the sound of it spooling up ahead of the bulkhead, the engine revving – this was so special, so Saab. It made overtaking manoeuvres safe. You simply checked for the gap, mirror, look over the shoulder, signal, get clearance, and having already dropped to third and pressed the power pedal

to anticipate the spool-up, the 900 Turbo then launched itself up the road in a surge of performance to whisk you past the traffic in style and utter safety. In a few seconds, you were gone, flying up the road at a rate of acceleration that even Porsche could not match. This became the art of Saab Turbo driving. It really was amazing for the money. No wonder it levitated Saab into a whole new world.

The 99 Turbo had done likewise but with perhaps a touch less gravitas; add water-injection and the results were of even higher supercar performance

Jean-Francois Bouvard shot his lovely 900 Turbo three-door flat-front Turbo in the French Alps.

standards. But 900 was about more than the turbo, even if that model headed its range and its aura.

From the mid-1980s, the 8 valve and then the 16 valve 900s breathed cleaner, had advanced technology ignition and combustion systems and intercooled turbochargers. The 1985 Saab Great Britain 25th Anniversary was marked by the rare 'Tjugofem' models with special equipment and decals (see photos). Saab Belgium produced the curious 1986 'Beverley' edition on a four-door 900 bodyshell with US-style alloys, leather trim and GLi engine specification.

I designed the bodykit for the 1985 British Saab Wimbledon 900 with its 'Sprint', and 'Sport' branded accessory option that included a full aerodynamic bodykit created under the auspices of Saab GB. This was the first Saab 900 bodykit.

Saab also offered the 900 with an interesting range of alloy wheels across its two decades of life, notably creating very attractive three-spoke alloy wheel deigns that are enthusiasts' favourites. In the 900, Saab carved a deeper brand legend and confirmed its place upon the world stage of car manufacturers of engineering integrity to be taken very seriously indeed.

9000

Saab went upmarket from the success of the 900 and created the 9000. Some people say it was a part-Fiat developed car and therefore not a 'real' Saab. I and many Saabists feel that this is unfair. True, Saab did a deal with Fiat to share the costs of developing a new large car. But the Saab version was filled with Saab specific design and engineering details created in Trollhattan by the true, core Saab team under Björn Envall's design lead. All the Saab details and ingredients were inherent within the Saab 9000. Great performance, brilliant seats and cabin comfort, safety, handling and style of an individual nature, it was all there. The car was a true Saab and drove like one and should not be categorised as a 'nearly' Saab.

Saab's management knew that it faced an issue, its cars had been on the market a long time and no knew Saab was in the pipeline. Saabs had never really been able to build enough cars in the volume numbers to support its high quality output and ethos.

A quick, yet effective solution was needed. Finance was the issue. The corporate connections between Saab and Fiat were not unknown; Saab had used an Italian engineering and design companies from Sixten Sason's time. Lancias had been sold in Sweden with Saab's help, as had the Autobianchi A112 small car. Lancia's top engineer Gianmario Rossignolo was friends with Saabs senior director Sten Wenlo and Saab's Georg Karnsund was pivotal in the Saab-Lancia relationship.

To cut a long corporate story short, Saab and Fiat talked and the outcome was the 'Type Four' project to jointly develop a new big car across these manufacturers' respective marques and specialisations. A deal was done via the influential Saab-backers the Wallenberg family with the Agnelli power base of Fiat. 1979 saw the plan signed off and a new big Saab (but not the vital a smaller one) was underway. The 9000 would be road-ready for testing in 1984 and launched in early 1985.

Ital Design shaped the Type Four design, but Saab's version was thoroughly re-worked by Envall into a recognisably Saab shape – although less curvaceous than previous Saabs. It was smart, modern, and looked like a fresh face for Saab. 9000, like 900 classic, started with an upright flat-front nose and was facelifted and given a slant-front nose.

Packed with substantial structural reinforcements, a unique front end crush-zone structure, roll-over protection and the wonderful Saab seats, the 9000 shared very little with the Fiat, Alfa Romeo and Lancia versions of the base unit. Only the roof skin and front door skin was common to the Saab from the Fiat and Lancia variants.

Not only did 9000 crash well in impact tests, it drove superbly – like a Saab should. 9000 topped the official American, and European, safety and crash test ratings and consumer listings. It was rated as Sweden's safest car from the 1980s to the 1990s.

9000 was fitted with a highly developed version of Saab's existing 16 valve engine and packed with emissions, anti-knock, and clean air technology amid its perfect turbocharger application. Transversely mounted, front driven and electronically controlled this was a 'thinking' engine that used world-leading emissions equipment to make it green and clean long before other car makers jumped on that bandwagon. Saab called its system APC – Automatic Performance Control.

Of note, the fuel-injection process used an early form of a stratified inject charge via microprocessor-controlled mechanism. Later 9000s would see a direct ignition (DI) type system with a coil for each cylinder. This was multi-spark technology.

The non-turbocharge 9000i with fuel injection was a version that many Saab buyers needed for a cheaper 9000 and it drove brilliantly. A four-door version soon arrived amid some level of design confusion with the old, flat-front styling being produced alongside certain models of the 9000 with the newer slant-front styling. A long-wheelbase limousine was also offered – as it had been for the classic 900. Sadly, no estate car version was offered, although Lancia did offer an estate version of its variant of the Type Four platform. So Saab missed a trick there.

A range of 9000 models as hatchbacks and saloons proliferated, some with larger engine capacity, some as 'Eco' specials. 'Carlsson' and 'Talledaga' special editions were launched, as was an 'Anniversary' or 'Jubilee' edition. The 'Griffin' versions used a four-door bodyshell and US-specific specifications were created for that market. The 9000 CS Aero used a different make of turbocharger as a departure from Saab's long standing supplier Garrett.

The famous and desired 'Aero' models spanned several iterations of 9000 styling and specifications. Sports suspension, body-kits, massive power increases and aerodynamic packages for US, global, and British markets became specific variants of the 9000. 9000 proved popular in Asia, but there were issues with heat-soak under the engine bay in tropical climes.

Ultimately, the heavily facelifted 9000 of 1991 onwards would see a top of the range Turbo 16S 'Aero' version of over 220bhp.

In 1992, the old, original 9000 MK1 bodyshell was sold in Sweden only as base model of lower trim specification at much lower cost. What a brilliant idea. In fact, two versions were marketed – a GLE and a lower-line CC.

The rear-end styling of the post-1992 9000 MkII was in most peoples' opinions a bit untidy, but there was no doubting that this was super Saab of immense appeal.

These CS-series cars had a lower front, higher tail, stronger doors, and were laden with advanced Saab-patented engine technology. From 1993, the 'Trionic' system was a Saab engine measuring and management device that actually measured ions to self-regulate the fuel/air combustion process via multiple electronic sensors. In inner-city traffic, the 9000's exhaust had fewer pollutants than the atmospheric air being sucked into the front of the car off the street! A Trionic T5 further developed the system using a direct injection cassette mechanism to manage the fuel-injection via multiple sensors and the throttle setting. T5 was not managed by a mass-airflow sensor to determine the pre-set mix.

The Trionic T7 again took development further advanced the engine's emissions excellence but used a torque-demand reactive programme to manage the system but via mass air sensor to react on-demand. The T7 control unit constantly tuned the turbocharger settings too. For a while, this was the world's most advanced engine management system, and it was of Saab design under Olle Granlund's lead.

High-pressure turbo models were complemented by lower-power low pressure turbo models. The 1997 2.3-litre 9000 full-pressure top oft eh range 9000 turbo delivered 330Nm of torque at just over 2,000rpm – no other car maker had achieved that efficiency with a turbocharged engine.

The 9000 MkII Aero was the fastest Saab ever built and top of its class performance to take on its rivals. It was a very characterful car and a true Saab. Tuners like MAPtune, and Abbott could coax 300bhp or more out of such a full-fat 2.3litre turbocharged engine.

It might be said that Saab got a bit carried away with the 9000's model badging nomenclature. After all, it was available as: T16, Injection, SE, CD, CDE, CDi, CS, CSE, CST, Aero Mk1, Aero MkII, GLE, CC, Griffin, and a range of special, named editions. American specifications were sometimes a mix and match of European or Swedish specifications.

9000 was built from late 1985 (launched early 1985) through to the last weeks of manufacture in 1997 prior to the new 9-5. Some cars were still in showrooms as 1998 dawned. 503,000 of the 9000 models were built in total. Many Saabists love the Saab 50th Anniversary edition with its Saab badges and 'propeller' motifs and high equipment levels.

9000 must have been Saab's most developed and 'improved' car model. 9000 was much underestimated by some, and surely must be seen as a 'real' Saab.

A gaggle of body-kitted 900 Turbo Carlssons with the Saab body kit seen at Swedish Day UK.

Chris Redmond's exquisite 900T flat-front three-door with the integrated bodykit as also seen on U.S.-spec 'SPG' cars. Note the rear extractor vent option amid classic Saab sculpture.

Above left and above right: Jean-Francois Bouvard's immaculate French registered 900T three-door captured in wonderful repose. Note the turbine-blade wheels as opposed to the Incas seen on the very early 900T.

900 Classicism as captured in this five-door with the extra windows in the C-pillar. Simple but highly effective as it powers up Prescott.

Above left: The same car captured in black and white. Saab purism.

Above right: The later 900T two-door with a boot/trunk panel and body kit really looked the part of the classic Envall-styled Saab.

Andy Murray in his hill-climb/track specification 900 flat-front Turbo named 'Everard'. What a lovely thing to do to an old 900 and make it drive.

Saab 16 Valve with associated pipework. Enough said.

Above left and above right: Simple is often best. Alex Rankin's two-door booted 900 shows off its design cues – note the very distinctive rear windscreen shape that Bjorn Envall added to the 900.

Left: Chris Redmond powers away in his classic 900T flat-front. It has the unusual maroon interior mouldings more commonly seen on certain export-spec and U.S.-spec 900s of the era. Smile, it's a Saab.

Right: Saab sculptures at rest. 900T and 99T.

Below left and below right: The British market special edition 'Tjugofem' edition 900 two-door eight valve was rare indeed and this one in almost as new condition reeks of Saab. Note the wheels off the 9000 MkI range! Tjugofem had spoilers, light infill décor panels, extra cabin kit and colour-keyed bits. Three hundred were made and celebrated 25 years of official Saab GB operations.

Above: The Tjugofem had a centre console with cassette racks. Note the narrow-depth curved windscreen, reverse curved fascia and aircraft cockpit design language.

Right: No blues here. Saab 16Valve engine and special air filter to make it breathe better.

Turbo classics captured with the clamshell bonnets open. Note the inner wing structure longerons that offered good full and overlap frontal impact performance.

16V and Malbrad tweaks as advertised. It goes. Steve Broadhead's Malbrad have been tuning Saabs for decades from a northern UK base.

Not quite so subtle but lovely nonetheless, this 900 convertible just oozes Saab intent.

Classic C900 Cabriolet shows off the increased A-pillar rake and clean styling. Such an elegant car.

This is why people love Saabs: sheer open motoring joy in a C900 Turbo convertible: proper driving with no digital authority to deal with.

Inside the cabriolet cockpit. Pure, utter Saab character.

Above left: C900T in Odorado Grey and seething with intent. This is a Saab club member's pride and joy. The number plate identifies him as Ellie Wilson, Saab club stalwart.

Above right: Slant-nose 900s came in from the 1987 model year and featured a neater bumper valance too. The 16V was launched worldwide too.

Above left and above right: Martin Lyons is a well-known Saabist and dedicated Saab addict. This is his superb 900T 16V two-door restoration catching the setting sun. That rear wing was very Saab Turbo and has a significant aerodynamic effect and is not just for show.

Lovely Belgian C900 convertible captured at speed at Prescott. Nice number plate.

Above left: Late-model 900 convertible interior with an unusual steering wheel fitted.

Above right: This late model classic 900 Ruby model has been expertly restored down in Somerset and is well-known at Saab events. Note the body-coloured bumpers and TR Autos number plate – he gets everywhere! Late 1993 was the end of the line for the lovely classic 900 and they Ruby edition was a great way to sign it off. Shame the Ruby series cars' factory paint was seemingly susceptible to damage.

Left: Swedes at the wheel: well-known American Saabist and writer Mark J. McCourt took this photo of Fredrik Nyblad driving an American-registered classic 900 cabrio with none other than Claes Johansson (of *Klassiker* magazine) in the passenger's seat. Fredrik and Claes publish and write the brilliant *Saab Cars* periodical to great acclaim as one of the great tributes to Saab. The pair got Mark to source this Talledaga red 900 for a road-trip up the U.S. East Coast – the old, original Saab USA hinterland of radicals, liberals, free-thinkers, rally-drivers, and 'different' people.

Opposite below: Classic Saab elegance personified as a three-door 900T scythes around Prescott at the Saab Club National when it made a very successful Prescott visit for its annual festival. The three-spoke wheels with grey spokes on silver rims look wonderful.

Above left: The slant-nose- added by Saab from late 1987 improved the aerodynamics and the looks. The body kit did likewise and was seen worldwide. Turbo S 16V.

Above right: This full-fat Turbo S has the very rare Saab rear windscreen cover accessory. Not pretty, but certainly effective – as is the larger rear spoiler that is of positively Porsche proportions.

Above and right: A 900 resprayed in bright sky blue metallic, THE 16S looked great and shows what can be done by the Saab enthusiast who is prepared to think laterally.

Seen in profile in white, 900 looks even bigger – as does that massive rear hatch door as seen here open.

The classic cabriolet or 'vert' seen alongside the five-door variant. Note the differing wheel designs and the 'square' booted rear end on the two-door shell of the cabriolet. Envall's rear lamp panel design as applied on the two-door, four-door and cabriolet was especially neat.

Above and opposite: Classic grey 900T powers away past the camera on a misty Welsh day at the Dragon Saab gathering. The character of the classic 900 is conveyed in these shots.

Above: Across the ages of Saab design language. Early 900 seen with alter 9-5 and 9-3.

Right: Turbo in the landscape. Saab sculpture.

4

From 9000 to 9-3 & 9-5: Different Saab

A later series 9000 with the revised post-1992 'CS'-type bodywork seen during the author's drive through western France. Alain Rosset's car had nearly 300bhp and a somewhat boost-laden character. With more space and more bulk, this was a big Saab car and it found many friends in the USA.

You might argue that the post-General Motors Saab's were not 'pure' Saabs but how far do you want to take purity and, what are you going to be a purist about? After all, did not the Saab 96 V4 use a Ford engine? Had not *other* car manufacturers bits and pieces found their way into the original 92 prototype? Both of the two-stroke engines that Saab had used in the 1950s had German origins. Saab's early aircraft had German, British and American origins. The Saab 9000 had been co-developed with Fiat, but it was a true Saab in all its engineering, design, and driving.

Perhaps we should not be too purist about the GM-era Saabs, and yet, they did lack that 100 per cent hewn from solid feel of an old Saab. They steered and went well, the turbocharged cars were excellent, yet the fit and finish was not of the old classic 900. But that approach with all its inherent costs, had cost Saab dear and indeed left Saab financially vulnerable.

The 'new' 900 of 1994 was Envall-influenced and a really accomplished piece of modern Saab design language: every line, every curve and ellipse seem to work and gel into a great piece of scaled Saab sculpture. The car was also developed and tweaked by Erik Carlsson and he tried to get the vital mechanical driving dynamics to feel like a Saab not an Opel/Vauxhall of GM provenance. But the truth was, although the new 900 and its subsequent facelift as the first 9-3 looked like a Saab and had all the Saab hallmarks amid its design language, it was not a 'pure' Saab in its DNA, and you could tell.

A V6 version was a paradox to the Saab four-cylinder turbocharging ethos of efficiency, yet was actually rather a good car and nice drive. This was a 2.5-litre GM-sourced six-cylinder that appealed notably in America. Other new 900s retained the well-developed Saab four-cylinder engine range with their smooth mechanism and instant responses from lower down the rev range. An electro-mechanical clutch semi-auto of 'Sensonic' branding would also be offered as an automatic.

Envall-designed, with influence in its later development by British Saab designer Simon Padian, the new 900 and the 9-3 it was facelifted into, used the base platform and under-the-skin toolings of the GM Opel/Vauxhall Calibre and Vectra base unit 'chassis' unit. But Saab went to town 'Saabising' all that they could.

Of particular note was the interior and dashboard design by Aina Nilsson, for this really was a top-notch Saab interior.

The new-generation 900 lasted from 1994 to 1998, thence to be structurally strengthened after a surprisingly poor EURONCAP crash test performance, facelifted and re-born as the 'new' 9-3 with over 1,000 improvements. Two types of diesel engine were offered with a 2.2Tid being a later addition that did not like drinking cheap, dirty diesel – but then, who would?

The high-powered, TWR-developed 'Viggen' sub-brand version was of course a true Saab in performance terms and came in a range of great colours and trims. Developed by Peter Leonard under the Saab Special Vehicle Operations department, the new Viggen was quick, almost too quick.

The special Viggen-type alloy wheels turned out to be somewhat soft, however. Viggen could also be bought as a cabriolet – which the new 900/9-3 Mk1 had invoked in memory of the classic 900 soft-top. Viggen boasted 173kW/ 239bhp and a Mitsubishi turbocharger system. 0-60mph took 6.3 seconds – real performance. Torque steer was an issue, but a special after-market brace could reduce it. So powerful was the Viggen that its gearbox needed protecting by an electronic, torque-sensing mechanism. 4,600 9-3 Viggens were built.

We should note that Abbott Racing in the U.K. had built a tuned-up high-performance version of the new 900 in 1994 with 235bhp from the Saab 2.0-litre turbo engine. They added traction control revised suspension and a limited slip differential. Did Saab create the subsequent Viggen from Abbott's inspiration? You might wonder.

These new Saab 900 and 9-3 cars were attractive and sold well, but despite the best efforts of Trollhattan, and an often ignored rallying and racing record, they were to define a new era of a different Saab. But we bought them, and they have now become modern classics. Just watch out for rust at the rear end.

When the next 9-3 Mk2, the second generation, was designed and built for the 2003 model year, GM were stricter about the expensive Saab-type additions that the Saab team wanted to add to the basic GM-supplied car platform. Again, Saab tried it on and to some degree succeeded. 9-3 Turbo X was a 211kW. 280bhp V6, turbo, all-wheel-drive of significant performance, a Saab in the finest of Saab tradition. Saab's Johansson-designed four-wheel drive clutch as a Haldex 'XWD' adaptable four-wheel-drive drivetrain with its self-sensing, self-modulating electronic limited slip differential, was world class and a fantastic device, a real technical achievement so typical of Saab.

The lower-line 1.9Tid engine 9-3 of multiple corporate engineering heritage beyond Saab, did not however, define what had been that certain Saabness.

9-3 series 2 or MKII, was strong and safe and had performance, it was also available as an estate car. The petrol-engined version went well and developed a following: the 1.9Tid diesel engine developed a reputation for problems, and the later cars of any engine type had low-quality cabin trim materials, notably the leather seat coverings which wore out in under 5,000 miles of normal use on the driver's seat. Plastics, mouldings, and materials all seemed less than Saab-like. Yet these cars sold, and the massive performance of the Turbo X range and the four-wheel drive application made many friends.

From 'Linear', 'Arc', 'Vector', to 'Aero', 9-3 had various trim names and specifications across the global market.

Simon Padian the Saab designer facelifted the cars for 2008 and a characterful new frontal design was created. For 2009, the four-wheel-drive estate version with a petrol engine refreshed the range, yet this niche Saab product was on the wane, as was Saab itself, and it showed in the cars and the lower-quality fittings. One of the more interesting versions of the car was the twin-turbocharged TTid, diesel which had good economy and stunning performance, but the serpentine yards of its synthetic drive belt looked like it could be expensive to live with.

For 2011-2012, 9-3 MkII got another revamp under the Saab Spyker ownership. Engine emissions were lowered and the diesel TTid got below the benchmark 120g C02 figure – a big achievement for a diesel engine.

9-5

During the development of the Type Four car as the 9000 as part of the joint venture with Fiat, it became clear that the Alfa Romeo version of the project would have its own unique bodyshell and one created at much greater expense than the bodyshell proposed for the Fiat, Lancia and Saab variants. Saab, of course, effectively reinvented their version at their own expense, but the Alfa 164, as it became, was radically different in styling and its outer skin.

At Saab, they wondered if Fiat and Saab could further develop the Alfa 164 into a big four-door saloon for Saab use. So was born the idea for the next new Saab – one born from the Alfa 164 that was the outcome of the Type Four project as a sort of reverse-engineered Fiat-Alfa-Saab saloon – not a hatchback.

This was the new Saab that died when GM, not Fiat, bought Saab – so died a fresh model due down the Trollhattan Saab pipeline. Yet Saab then created a booted, saloon version our of the existing 9000! GM had also created a link-up with Fiat at this time. A confused situation developed. But Saab still needed a new car for the late 1990s and beyond.

GM supplied the base floorpan and tooled underpinnings from within its own range of Vectra models. This became Saab's project 640 as new Saab saloon. The body style was directed by Einar Hareide. Tony Catignani was also on the 95 styling team. Ingrid Karlsson led the interior design team. Other Saab interior and general design names of the 1990s included: Cynthia Charwick, Aina Nilsson, and Maria Thunberg. Bryan Nesbitt, Anders Gustaffson, Simon Padian, and Ralph Jonsson contributed to the Saabness of things.

Haken Danielsson was the aerodynamics man. Despite being a booted-saloon, the 9-5 controlled airflow along and off its rear body very well and had a low CD 0.29, to CD 0.31, in full production trims, and a low wake vortex drag, with good side wind stability.

Using design elements form the original 99 and 900, notably the swept rear and curved front windscreen and roof turret, 9-5 was a fantastic new view of Saab design language without being a retro-pastiche.

The new 9-5 was a class leader in terms of passive safety as crash-safety, it incorporated special side-intrusion members, a clever impact management structure in the B-pillar, and very good load paths in the front crush zone to control head-on and offset frontal crash forces to limit cabin intrusion. Mats Fägerhag led the new car's safety systems developments and the 9-5 led the global and EURONCAP safety and test rankings for a long time. 9-5 also had Saab's new active-head restraint which incorporated a mechanism to significantly reduce head and neck injuries in rear-end accidents. Such was typical Saab concern for personal safety.

Leif Larsson was the 9-5's drivetrain and suspension engineer and the whole project was overseen by Saab veteran Olle Granlund, a man who knew what a Saab should be.

Designed from 1994 onwards and ready in remarkably short development time, the new big Saab was to be called 9-5 and equipped with the usual range of advanced Saab engines. A GM-sourced diesel was also offered, initially as a rare 3.0-litre turbo diesel. Smaller capacity diesel engines would latterly be fitted – right down to the 1.9Tid. An asymmetrically turbocharged petrol V6 was technically interesting for the 9-5 alongside the normal Saab 2.0-litre turbocharged engines.

Launched in late 1997, 9-5 was a big hit and appealed not just to traditional Saab owners, but attracted many new fans to the Saab badge.

Of note, the 9-5 was also offered as handsome estate car that proved very popular. And the 2.3-litre so-called 'Hot' Aero-specified versions of both saloon and estate were real performance cars and had an over-boost function controlled by computer that delivered extra overtaking urge when required. With 191kW/256bhp on tap, the top-of-the-range 9-5s were very powerful and very desirable: over-boost could briefly deliver 270bhp. At the other end of the scale, the 'Bio-power' blended fuel model addressed environmental concerns.

The infamous engine 'sludge' problem manifested and, in 2004, Saab made changes to alleviate its occurrence in the engines oiling system.

In 2002, a styling and specification and trim revision was undertaken, then in 2006 a third facelift with radical and controversial front-end styling occurred. The original interior was re-finished with more modern materials yet using the original fascia and trim mouldings. Somehow, 9-5 had been modernised for a new era. But the fact was that, once again, Saab was selling a good, but old car amid truly new cars to be found in rival makers' showrooms. Good as 9-5 was, after a decade it became a harder sell. By mid-2009, the saloon had died, leaving the estate 9-5 to struggle on until the arrival of the new 9-5 for another year on sale. 483,583 units of all the 9-5 types were sold. 9-5 had Saabness within it, but the GM influence was increasingly felt. 9-5 also developed rear-end rust – just like the 900 Mk2/9-3 Mk1. A legacy of something in the process of GM-to-Saab perhaps?

Last chance saloon?

From late 2009 to Saab's demise nearly three years later the new, 9-5 Mk2 made many friends.

Wonderfully styled in perhaps the most evocative Saab design language seen for years, the new GM-based car continued the traditions of Saab individualism despite the bean-counters of GM hovering over it. Using the GM/Saab 'Epsilon' platform, and based over the Opel Insignia's framework, the new 9-5 shouted Saab. In fact very few GM/Opel parts were left on view. 9-5 Mk2 boasted a fantastic 'cockpit' design interior and you knew you were in a Saab. This car was no trick, nor a trade-off. 9-5's styling was timeless and beyond fashion. Naturally, you could buy a new 9-5 equipped with everything from small 1.9-litre diesel engine: a potential 1.6-litre engine, to a V6 four-wheel-drive powerhouse. The bigger, 143kW/190bhp TTid engine worked well in the new 9-5. Sadly, problems with the 4x4 drivetrain were not unknown. The lovely, illuminated rear lamp panel on the tailgate also failed regularly. Cabin trim also seemed fragile. Stop-start production and supplier issues may have had a negative effect on 9-5 build quality say some observers.

Hirsch, the performance accessory people, had tweaked up 9-5 Mk1 and offered extras for 9-5Mk2. By 2011, production issues and corporate issues had manifested amid Saab, but some 9-5s were produced with a two-tone interior treatment that really enhanced the cabin. Other various specification tweaks were brought in

Launched in late 2009 at Frankfurt Motor Show, there followed the promise of the 'Combi' estate car version that was deemed to be the best looking estate car for years. Sadly, its production life was effectively still-born by the turmoil of the sale of Saab amid the GM and Spyker events. A few, a very few new 9-5 Mk2 estates escaped!

10,000 new 9-5 Mk2 were built, before the end of Saab. In America, new 9-5s sat forlornly in storage, as they did in Europe.

What happened amid the GM-sell off and Spyker/Muller's well-intentioned effort to save Saab, is legend. There is no need to recount it here. Except to say that you might be surprised to learn how much GM learned and took from Saab despite never using Saab in the manner that lay behind GM's purchase of it in the first place.

So died Saab.

Saab, one of the most intelligent and cleverest car makers as the purveyor of character cars of quality and a unique philosophy, ended.

A part of Swedish history has gone. And Volvo is Chinese owned now. Somehow it still seems unbelievable, but the truth is that the men in suits from the corporates, notably the big ones, oversaw the death of a marque and end of a philosophy. The Swedes ought to own up to a percentage of the blame for being so paradoxical – free-thinking, yet stuck in their ways at the same time. But others, further afield should have known better.

There is no point is moaning any more. Another Saab company still makes aircraft, but the separated- off Saab car company does not make Saabs but in its new iteration by another name, has an electrical intent as a new brand. The Saab car brand name floats in limbo. Perhaps we should just celebrate one of the greatest stories of automotive engineering and industrial design that ever travelled the earth. Its name was Svenksa Aeroplan Aktiebolaget – S.A.A.B.

Tak sy mycket Saab

Above: The revised 9000 kept the doors and glass of the original, but featured a reinforced C-pillar, new rear hatch and windscreen and several frontal styling iterations. Thoroughly engineered by Saab, this was indeed a 'proper' Saab and a great car.

Opposite: Dials, wood, leather, and ergonomics – the later 9000 interior.

Above: One of the later-series 9000's less successful design elements was the rear lamp and valance panel.

Right: The CS-type rear end incorporated an attempt at classic Saab rear-pillar design language with a swept curve.

Left: Those 'Aero' type seats were judged to be Saab's best-ever seats.

Opposite above: The earlier 9000 body but with the slant-nose as applied in 1991 after being first seen on the saloon version only from late 1988. This is what to do with an old 9000 – make it into a track day car! Lewis Turner at the helm of his T25 turbocharger B202-engined 9000 of 230bhp and a touch of Nitro! Oh, and it's lost 250kg in weight too – the car not the driver.

Opposite below: The booted 9000 CDE. 2/3-litres, direct injection DI, double balance shafts, overhead camshafts, sixteen valves, turbocharged, and with Trionic latterly added, were all later 9000 items, as was a three-litre V6! The variations of engines and bodies were getting rather confusing. Trim tags ranged from CC, CD, CDi, CSE, CDE, Turbo, Turbo 16S, 'Carlsson', 'Aero', 'Griffin': the 'Griffin' version was both luxurious and powerful.

Envall's elegant 9000 morphed into the later series which gained profile worldwide. The 200bhp 'Aero' version of 1997 was the fastest-ever Saab. The 'Celebration' 9000 models of 1997 marked Saab's 50th Anniversary and looked great in dark metallic blue.

Above left: Another early 9000 2.3T as track day car, with the body kit (as also seen on Carlsson version) fitted. This is the SGB Racing/Stephen Field car that was first in class in 2018's Classic touring Car Championship. This car has an enhanced cooling system (to also complement the Abbott intercooler) – not a bad idea for turbo at full pelt.

Above right: The 'new' GM 900 became the 9-3 but looked very similar. This 9-3 five-door sported the usual Saab body kit and lovely alloys. Somehow, elements of the old classic 900's styling were captured despite the GM underpinnings.

Right: The upswept Saab rear was retained but this was its last true iteration in the 9-3 Mk1.

Classic Saabism captured. Light falling on the Saab sculpting proves that the styling was successful.

Right: The 'new' 900 saw Saab rap its style over the GM under platform. The three-door captured the classic 900 line very well. Available with a smooth GM V6 and the 'Sensonic' electro-mechanical semi-automatic gearbox that aped the old Sax-O-mat device. The new 900 became the 9-3 with over 1,700 modifications. This is Mark McCourt's American spec 9-3 coupe in a very nice Saab green.

Below: Here is the same bodyshell but revised and strengthened into the 9-3. Was this the last iteration of the old Saab wing profile style?

Left: ALU 36 was one of Saab's most popular and effective later alloy wheel designs.

Right: More modern Saab branding saw the post Saab-Scania branding evolve into the Saab 'wing' bar on the grille and a griffin on the badge.

Below left: Modern Classic in the form of a 900 -9-3 new-generation cabriolet seen at Bristol Gliding Club – gliders being an old Saab press photo favourite.

Below right: One of the best bits about the new 900 and 9-3 GM cars was the fantastic Saab-themed aircraft-inspired dashboard and interior.

Above: Viggen and its badge became a Saab de facto sub-brand in the story of the new generation 9-3. 230bhp and a Mitsubishi TD04 turbocharger with Trionic made it rather quick. The idea for the car was developed by Peter Leonard who worked with TWR to develop the Viggen. But was it all inspired by Abbott Racing who built a tuned-up ARMT-16 three-door new-model 900 Turbo with 235bhp with revised suspension and a limited slip differential. Saab's Special Vehicle Operations division studied that car. Viggen followed.

Right and below: Viggen cabriolet at speed at Prescott. Viggen Blue not Cosmic Blue if you please. Those original Viggen alloys were somewhat 'soft'. Note the rear 'bridge' spoiler.

Above: A few Viggens were sold not in blue but in Monte Carlo Yellow. These cars really are now modern classics and despite the GM platform, are deemed to contain enough of the spirit of Saab design to be accepted as collectors' items.

Opposite: 9-3 Mk2 in Cerulean Blue with the hood up; still a stylish Saab and a car with a dedicated following. Again, Saab went to town on the alloy wheel design.

Above left and above right: The second-generation 9-3 was a saloon not an upswept Saab hatchback coupé. The author drove this one through Tasmania and it had the TTID engine which was superb. At least the clamshell bonnet – a Saab motif was obvious. The Saab team did all they can to give the car some Saab style. Saab designer Simon Padian influenced the later 9-3s and 9-5s.

Left: It might be modern, but this is clearly a Saab and a modern classic in the form of another 9-3 cabriolet.

Opposite: The 9-3 Mk2 included the excellent estate or 'wagon' version – or 'Combi' if you are Swedish. Last-of-the-line Saab styling really gave it some presence and stemmed from the Turbo X special.

Left: If you are a Saab fan and want a modern car, then this 9-3 Mk2 and the last 9-5, are your only choice. Years after the death of Saab, this 9-3 is still a good looking car in a modern content.

Below and opposite: 'Turbo X' of 2008 let Saab's engineers and designers off the hook and delivered a true performance Saab in the modern era. Turbo X had 280bhp, from its 2.8-litre turbocharged V6 with a wall of power and torque on tap. The Saab-Haldex XWD four-wheel-drive system was self-monitoring and had a 'take-off' (and a limited slip differential) programme to reduce wheel slip. A body kit and more amazing Saab alloy wheel design really gave the black Turbo X real character.

Opposite above left: 9-5 from the closing days of the 1990s was an Einar Hariede design. The car was the outcome of a second attempt at a new big Saab after a previous project (as a reverse-engineered Fiat) had foundered amid Saab's corporate issues at the time. The outcome of 'Project 640' was the 1997 launch of the 9-5 with Einar Hariede, Tony Catignani, as styling leads with Ingrid Karlsson working on the interior, and Haken Danielsson engineering the car's superb aerodynamics and Mats Fagerhag sorting the car's class leading crash safety structure. Arne Nabo worked on the 'cockpit2 ergonomics. Olle Granlund was the project manager. Traditional Saab design elements were mounted on a GM platform, but this was a highly characterful Saab that would evolve across several facelifts during over a decade on the market.

Opposite above right: French Saab fans loved their new 9-5s and this one has the body kit and wonderful alloys.

Opposite below: The view seen under an enthusiast owner's 9-5 bonnet.

Above: Turbo X themes filtered down to the final restyles of the 9-3 prior to the demise of Saab. Yellow might be a bit bold, but the cabriolet looked great in this colour. Both these cars captured the final spirit of Saab.

Right: Mr and Mrs Glander are stalwarts of Saabs, the Saab Enthusiasts Club and usually appear in a white 96 V4, but shocked us all with their new family steed – a yellow 9-3 cabriolet.

Saabist Robin Morley blacked out the A-pillars on his 9-5 wagon and it worked! Note the later nose styling as it rushes up Prescott hill: an individual Saab for sure.

The estate and the saloon versions of 9-5 still have a major following as Saabs of the modern classic era. The car on the right has the Mk2 nose job.

Above left: Saab smiling: a 9-5 with a 'Saabs United' registration plate. Saabs United was Steven Wade's famous Saab blog that was born from its Trollhattan Saab origins.

Above right: Left too long on the market by force of fate, the 9-5 gained the infamous 'Dame Edna' facelift at the front. We are not sure what Dame Edna thought about it though…

Right: Here captured was the styling that hinted at the traditional Saab 'hockey stick' upswept bodyline of the old 99 and classic 900. The elliptical door handles were a rather nice touch.

Above and opposite: Last of the line 9-5 saloon captured coming and going in all its essential Saabness. Saab purists may disagree, but this is a Saab, just a different sort of Saab.

Above and left: The sad Saab years of 2009-12 say the end of Saab just as a brilliant new 9-5 arrived. But corporate machinations amid the GM sell-off and a raft of issues stemming from many sources, precluded Mr Muller taking Saab to his intended new heights. Simon Padian's living evocation of Saab design language manifested in the new 95. Sadly, the car and its wonderful estate-car or 'wagon' version, succumbed to what happened to Saab. This silver sculpture belongs to British Saabist Robin Morley. If you are lucky you might spot a top-of-the-range high-power V6 XWD version but they remain rare.

Opposite above: Silver Swedes at rest. Little did they know the fate of Saab, but the car on the left (then owned by former Saab Owners Club man Mike Philpott) appeared on *Top Gear*.

Opposite below left: Saab made great wheels to the end. This is their last 'turbine' incarnation in alloy.

Opposite below right: Saab 92 seen with the nose of a new 9-5. Somehow they both speak of Saab.

Tears for the end of Saab. A Fjord Blue 9-5 rests in Europe near the end of our Saab times. Saabist Robin Morley stopped to capture this evocative image –upon which we fittingly end our Saab memorial.

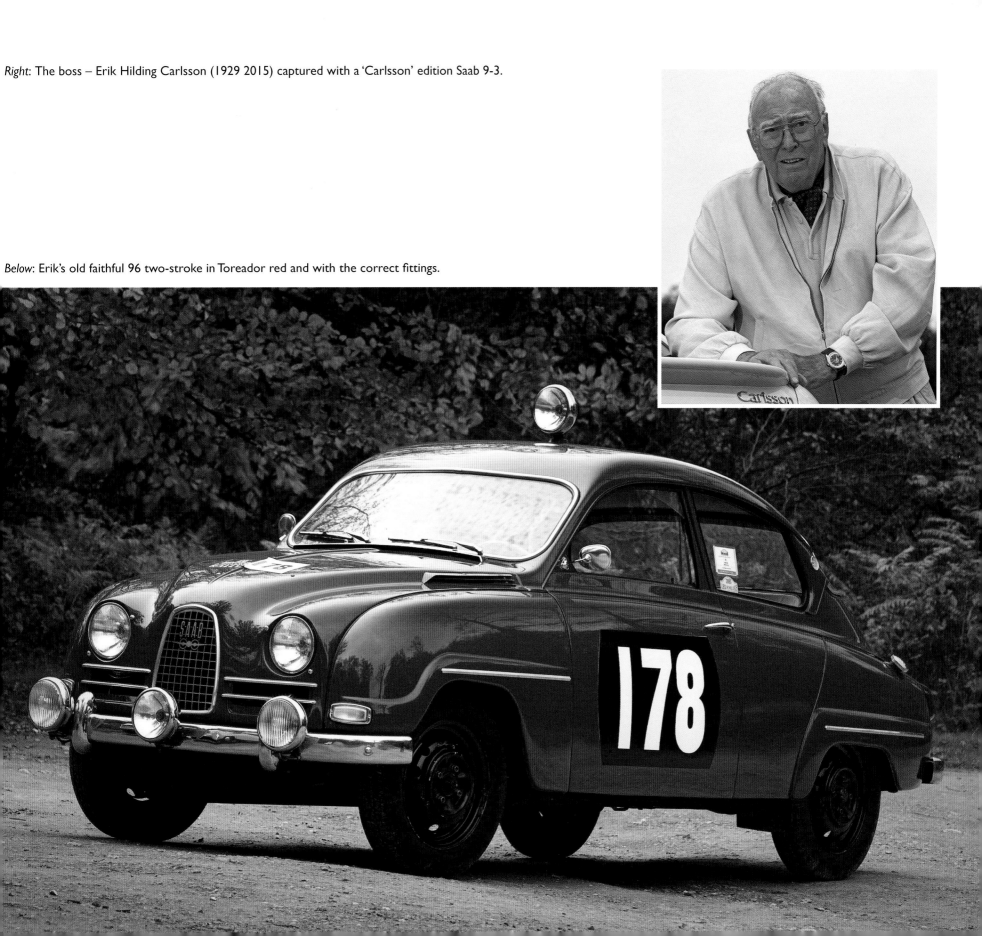

Right: The boss – Erik Hilding Carlsson (1929 2015) captured with a 'Carlsson' edition Saab 9-3.

Below: Erik's old faithful 96 two-stroke in Toreador red and with the correct fittings.

Index